S0-ASK-269

Monday Memo:
Creating Change in Early Childhood Education, One Message At A Time

ISBN: 978-0-9815587-9-0

Copyright © 2014 DJ Schneider Jensen, All Rights Reserved

Cover Design © DJ Schneider Jensen

Published by
Rocking R Ventures, Inc.
Epworth, GA

www.rockingrventures.com

FOREWARD

Dr. Lillian Englund

To: DJ

From: Lillie

Date: A Moment in Time

Re: Monday Memo

Dear DJ,

Today I read your entire book in one sitting. What a wonderfully crafted journey through the process of becoming a developmentally appropriate early childhood professional ... a journey that the best among us can relate to (and smile about) and the novices in our ranks can benefit from as you become their own private mentor. Through it all your special gifts as a teacher, director, mentor, friend, and entertainer shine as remarkably as the Northern Lights.

You touched on so many roles that we all perform in our classrooms and programs. You explain through example and anecdote how each of our roles affect, impress, and imprint a child to model our behavior and learn from us both appropriate and inappropriate behaviors. You carefully delineate the reasons for why our own experiences as children in our own classrooms affect our beliefs about teaching. Monday Memo demonstrates how careful reflection can help us to become better educators.

The most impressive gift from reading this book is the full understanding of the value of developmentally appropriate practice to the growth of a young child who is growing toward personal independence. Each developmental domain is addressed through example. When a child is taught through developmentally appropriate methods, the life-time affects of that teaching and the child's understanding of the greater community are showcased. When a child is taught through inappropriate methods, the portrait of poor behavior, withdrawal, and a lack of sense of purpose are graphically explained.

You shared with us who you are. The thread throughout regarding your sister as well as your memos to your Mom and fellow director teach us that we can only positively influence our colleagues when they know who we are. Within professional boundaries, you let the readers glimpse your personal interests and concerns and demonstrate the same caring and concern for them that you have for children. Monday Memo is a developmentally appropriate teaching method for early childhood educators. It is also a great resource for parents in understanding the sometimes hazy concepts surrounding child-directed curriculum.

Importantly, Monday Memo is an enjoyable read with enough professional jargon to illustrate your experience and education in the field without overwhelming the warmth of your personal style. It is well referenced, and contains additional tools for educators to use on a daily basis.

I am proud to have it in my collection.

Love,
Lillie

Preface

Leadership and Learning
are indispensable to each other. – John F. Kennedy

Thank you for reading Monday Memo! You are holding over 25 years of experience condensed into close to 200 pages. This includes 25 years of running a preschool, motivating teachers, educating parents, and creating change. Twenty-five years of trial and error, which, along with the guidance of my mentors, brought me to a place where I can speak to parents and teachers with confidence. Twenty-five years that crafted my vision of an ideal preschool. I am grateful to have the opportunity to share my ideas and strategies with you. Thank you for giving me the chance!

Many many years ago I was a Preschool Director in Las Vegas, Nevada. On my very first day I spilled a cup of coffee all over myself just as a new parent came into my office, anxious about starting start her two year old. I was soaking wet and mortified. And my brand new blouse! Being my mother's daughter and covered in hot coffee, a stream of inappropriate and colorful words came flying out of my mouth.

On the second day, I had unscheduled visits from both child care licensing and the health department. It appears that this same mother, horrified by something she heard from her son's teacher, called in two complaints. The visit from licensing yielded three pages of changes that had to be made within 30 days.

On the evening of the second day, I called the owner of the school, begging him to let me quit. He told me no. He did, however, offer me an additional 50 cents an hour if I stayed.

Thanks, Mr. Ron. Smart move.

Fast forward to 2011. I've been training preschool teachers and directors across the United States for more than two decades. Oftentimes I am asked, "Can you just write down what you say to parents (or teachers)? It makes so much sense when you say it, but I can never remember it when I need it." (Oh, the irony! If they only knew the words I spewed my very first day!)

I wrote Monday Memo to share my philosophy of creating change. The story takes place in a fictional school where I am the director. If you can suspend reality and imagine with me, I can teach you a great deal.

Join me as I lead Northern Lights Preschool into the world of developmentally appropriate practice, emergent learning, teacher-child partnerships, and meaningful family involvement. Along the way I face teachers who tell me one thing and do another, parents who are concerned about academic outcomes, and staff who are new to the idea of DAP. (Sound familiar?)

Monday Memo: Creating Change in Early Childhood Education, One Message at a Time

For the sake of this book I communicate in notes, weekly Monday Memos, letters to teachers, parents, my mom, and my colleague and confidant, Beth. As a general rule, I would not communicate with my teachers in letters. These notes are really just models of how those conversations (and self talk) would go.

The script-like conversations represent the times you are walking down the hall and hear 'hey-boss-do-you-have-a-sec?' Usually what follows is important, or challenging, or even uncomfortable, not unlike driving in your car and hearing your son in the back seat ask, "How did I get in your tummy, Mommy?"

In the appendices you'll find a bibliography, more notes and a list of discussion questions for a community of practice to use in a book club. Thank you for believing in the inherent value of early childhood education, and taking the steps to continued excellence!

If you'd like to share your stories with me, my email is playforaliving@gmail.com. I look forward to hearing from you!

Enjoy!

Acknowledgements

"Man only learns in 2 ways – one by reading and the other by association with smarter people." - Will Rogers

To: Quite possibly everyone I've ever met
From: DJ
Date: Today
Re: With gratitude

To Dan and Nick, who taught me everything by simply being my sons. Thank you.

To the teachers, administration and owners of programs for which I've given professional development over the past 26 years, I offer my sincere appreciation.

To the schools for which I've been director; I offer thanks to every teacher, parent, child and lay leader. Your faith in me gave me the courage to push the envelope and shape my vision.

To my colleagues across the United States and abroad, namely NJECN and ALLIANCE members, I thank you for taking me and my crazy thoughts seriously, and for seeing me as an equal long before I saw myself as one.

To the local Baltimore JPLAY schools, and all their wonderful teachers, thank you for trying out my ideas and offering feedback along the way. I am fortunate that you've shared your journey with me these past nine years, and allowed me to help you grow your practice.

Special thanks to Rachael Schwartz, Zac Price, Michelle Gold, Renee Stadd, Brenda Schuman, Ilene Vogelstein, Rachel Perry, Aileen Friedman, Zippora Schorr. Thank you, Joyce Harris, for introducing me to William.

To my coworkers at the Center for Jewish Education: You inspired me to continue reading and studying. Special thanks to Larry Ziffer, Leora Pushett and Miriam Cotzin Burg for supporting my ongoing pursuit of learning.

A world of gratitude to Lillian Englund, Mara Bier, Melissa Lebowitz and Randi Albertsen for your friendship. You each are an unending source of information and I'm lucky to know you.

This book is in your hands specifically because of two people: Dr. Edyth Wheeler, who suggested I write this as an independent study, and Dr. Tim Rice, my ever patient publisher who helped mold my thoughts into a coherent piece of work. Thank you for believing in my vision.

My biggest debt of thanks belongs to Jon, my remarkable husband of 26 years, who encouraged me to never stop learning and always keep teaching.

For my first and best friend, Cheryl Schneider Carter.

I love you sister.

Welcome to
Northern Lights Preschool!

When dealing with people, remember you are not dealing with creatures of
logic, but creatures of emotion. -Dale Carnegie

Dear Mom,

I feel like I'm in the middle of paradise. As I write this, I am sitting under a tree in a small field of grass and flowers. There's a bird walking past me, and I can feel the sun beating down. What a wonderful way to spend an afternoon! In fact, this is going to be a wonderful way to spend many afternoons because it is actually the garden yard of my new school!

That's right! I got the job, and today is my first day as the director of Northern Lights Preschool! It's a small (there are 74 children) school in Burlington, VT; a beautiful school in a lovely diverse community. We found an apartment within walking distance from the college for Kevin. He's thrilled to be home working on his Ph.D, and I am so happy to have found a preschool with great potential. After 20 years of working in large programs, this will be a refreshing change of pace.

During my interview, the parents and board members told me that they were proud of their school and wanted to find a director who would make sure theirs was one of the best in the state. There are several good programs here; especially the one connected to UVM. I'm not certain the board knows what a great program really looks like. (They admitted they didn't know what it took to be one of the best, but they wanted it nonetheless.)

I can tell they value the teachers and administration. Even though the school is small, there is a full time secretary. The director before me retired—the dearly beloved founder. It's a little scary following the footsteps of the local legend that shaped this school. Thankfully, the hiring committee liked my vision or I wouldn't feel comfortable walking into this program. As you know, I couldn't lead a school that didn't share my vision.

There are two classrooms each for three and four year olds. There is also a class of older two year olds. I was told that some parents come to this school specifically for the fours program because the academic teachers prepare them for kindergarten. This was a red flag to me because I have different ideas about what it means to prepare children for kindergarten, and I don't subscribe to the kindergarten prep school mentality.

However, when I walked through this 100 year old schoolhouse, with its original moldings, tall windows, and hardwood floors, I instantly fell in love. There is a history here I want to be a part of. The school house was sold to a church back in the early 1940's and stayed that way until the parents in the community decided they wanted a neighborhood preschool in 1981. And now it's my turn to take the helm. I can't wait to start implementing my vision.

Each room has a lead and a co-teacher and there is one full-time floater. Last spring, the parents' committee designed and built this beautiful garden for the children. This fall will be the first time they will get to play out here.

The school has a small staff lounge and a nicely equipped kitchen with a full time cook. This school serves the children two snacks and a hot lunch. The old chapel is an ideal space for gross motor activities during the winter, plus it doubles as a social hall for family events.

Interestingly enough, this school has never gone through NAEYC accreditation. The former director felt they were just fine without the accreditation and no one challenged her. Since I am committing to make this school one of the best in the state, we will need to start working towards accreditation as soon as possible.

I'm looking forward to meeting the staff next week. Our first staff meeting is on Wednesday afternoon followed by several days for professional development before school begins. I hope to use that time to learn about their teaching styles and get to know how they view the child. I've learned over the past 25 years that if they see the child as a competent learner who deserves respect, we will do just fine. Otherwise, I'll have some work to do! I'm glad to have this garden to visit whenever I like. I consider myself very lucky.

I'll keep you posted.
I love you Mom!

A Note from DJ

August 13

Dear Beth,

Congratulations on your new job! That is wonderful news! Looks like both of us are moving on to new challenges.

Your school sounds great. 250 children? That's 5 times bigger than the little one you cut your teeth on! You may think that equates to five times the work, but it doesn't. It will be amazing. You are a wonderful director. You're ready for this.

From what you've told me, it looks like both of our schools are in for some changes. We both picked highly academic programs that want to be the best. We both have to teach our families and teachers how children learn and help them make the shift from teacher-controlled learning to teacher-child partnerships. Thankfully, we have each other to bounce off ideas!

It sounds like you have a great admin team and a good staff. It will take some time to get to know everyone. Remember that you can't make changes until you have buy in from some of your staff. Just take one step at a time and you will be fine! Remember, they are just as scared of you as you are of them!

I start on Monday. I will have a week or so to become familiar with Vermont regs and plan staff training before the teachers come in to set up their classrooms and meet for professional development. I plan to spend most of our fall training getting to know them and covering developmentally appropriate practice. The board's comment that the school has a reputation for academic excellence caught my attention. I have to teach them DAP.

The way I see things, Beth, is that there are many approaches to teaching, but two very strong strands:

There is the teacher who believes in giving information to the children. "This is a pumpkin. It is orange. Not blue. Not red. Orange. It is also round. See how it is round and not square? Pumpkin starts with P. Say Puh, puh, pumpkin. I have a story about a pumpkin. Listen to my story. Let's color our pumpkins orange and place pumpkin seeds on them." In this example, there is the APPEARANCE of learning (repetition), but little interest or excitement on the part of the child.

Then we have the teacher who believes in allowing the children to gain knowledge through their own experiences. For her, the experience begins with putting a pumpkin on a table and allowing the children to "check it out." It's through that process that one child will announce, "Hey, look a pumpkin!" When this happens, the excitement begins and the other children enter into a "lesson" from their peers. The teacher serves as a facilitator responding to questions like "Why is it so bumpy?" with answers like "What do you think made it bumpy?" The teacher will offer support as they open it up to see if the thing that made it bumpy is inside the pumpkin (I'm going with the connection that Mom was bumpy when baby sister was inside her, so is there a baby pumpkin inside this one?) In this example, learning is hands on and exciting. The children will want to share with their parents and friends their 'discoveries', which gives them a chance to repeat what they know, (in some cases that includes writing the word pumpkin), thereby reinforcing the learning almost immediately.

When teachers who practice the first plan hear about the second approach, they may react in a number of ways. For some, the news of a different approach is wonderful and something to be embraced immediately. For many, while the news of a different approach is intriguing, there is push back because the teacher is unsure how the child will reach all of today's learning goals.

In the second pumpkin example, the children will learn the word pumpkin in addition to seeing first hand what the pumpkin feels and smells like inside.

During their conversations, they will chat about it being a circle (round) and maybe compare the white and orange pumpkins.

What is missing, in the eyes of the first teacher, is the guarantee that every child will want to write the word pumpkin, thereby learning the letter P and the sound Puh. I think they are looking at it all wrong.

Think about an 18 month old who sorts through lemon and orange slices to find the one that tastes good. Or the two year old who see the golden arches and yells out "McDonald's!" Or the three year old who sees a stop sign and whispers to himself "STOP". These children are learning all by themselves prompted by the environments we offer them.

We both know that telling a teacher that she doesn't understand child development is professional suicide. My plan is to share my vision with the teachers, help them find a way to connect with this vision in a way that makes sense, and give them time and space to make the changes.

Keep me posted on your school. How are you planning to approach your new staff? Will you be a drill sergeant or a teddy bear? No need to rush into changes, just get to know them first. It's all about the relationships you build.

Here's to a great year!

DJ

Hi Mom!

I had my first staff meeting last night. What a fun group of people! We have 11 teachers and a cook. Everyone was warm and welcoming. I expected them to be nervous about potential changes, but for the most part they were positive and receptive to my ideas. Every classroom is named after an animal. Here's the rundown of the Northern Lights Preschool team.

Lambs: (Twos) Susan Baker and Barbara Daniels. Susan is new this year. She was an assistant at a local daycare and was hired at the end of last year when the former two's teacher moved out of state. She told me that she loves children and is a little nervous about this year. During the meeting, she was cutting out alphabet letters for the wall. I asked her if she had heard the term 'Routines as Curriculum' (which refers to using the three routines - eating, diapering and sleeping - as opportunities to teach necessary life skills). She looked really lost at that question. No worries. I can teach her.

Barb's been here for a few years as the assistant and told me right away that she didn't want to be a lead teacher. She shared right away that she loves being able to leave her job at work.

Monkeys: (Threes) Debra Cassidy and Emma Brindal. Debra, the lead, has worked with three year olds for 15 years. She has a calm demeanor and great confidence in her approach to teaching.

Emma is a sweet older French woman. What a lovely lady! She and I spoke French for a few minutes, and she was gracious enough to overlook my mistakes. I was surprised to hear that she doesn't speak French to the children. We need to take advantage of this opportunity. I can tell by her smile and warmth that she loves the children and her job.

Lions: (Threes) Jennifer Gray and Jacquie Golden. Jenn is the lead. I love love LOVE this team! They have been teaching together for 7 years. They are very funny girls who finish each other's sentences and laugh all the time. I think this will be a fun room to play in. I did notice a little red flag when the assistant, Jacquie, told me that she likes to work on the children's manners and listening skills. Teachers who focus on manners and listening skills with three year olds generally do so because they lack an understanding of what is developmentally appropriate for that age group.

Tigers: (Fours) Kathleen Witherington and Kaycee Dell. Mrs. Witherington ("Call me Mrs. W. It's much easier") has been at NLP for 20 years, and was a Kindergarten teacher before that. She's very kind, gracious and impeccably well dressed! She wore heels and pearls to the meeting. You can tell the staff respects her because they made comments like "Mrs. W. taught me so much about talking to the parents." or "Mrs. W. has all the great ideas!"

Kaycee has worked with Mrs. W. for three years. She's outgoing and funny and reminds me of Tina Fey. She graduated last year from UVM. She told me that Mrs. W. was her cheerleader when school got tough.

Bears: (Fours) Deirdre Knox and Grant Schuman. Deirdre has been at NLP for 12 years. She, too, is a sharp dresser and was wearing high heels and pearls. (I wondered if she and Mrs. W. call each other in the morning to see what the other is wearing.) Before everyone came to the meeting, she showed me a big binder filled with the worksheets and handouts she created. She said she loved how the children were all sponges and seemed to love to learn to read and write (implying, of course, that this happens while using her materials). I got the feeling she was letting me know that this is the way things are done in her world and the sooner I knew that, the better for all of us. I'm not sure about this one, Mom. She could be my challenge.

Thank goodness she has Grant! He is the comic relief in that room. What a fun guy! Tall, great head of hair, very smart, with a Jack Nicholson smirk on his face. Grant always has a funny comment. More importantly, he understands that children need time to explore materials and is an advocate for ECE. He 's working on a Master's degree at UVM in Education. He wants to be an elementary school principal, but I hope he never leaves!

There is a floater named Becca May. She is currently working on her Bachelor's degree in Education. She's young and quiet, and is respected by the others. Grant mentioned something about taking a trip to Aruba when he won the lottery, and commented that as long as Becca was here, he'd be fine leaving his "kids".

We have a cook! The last time I worked in a school with a cook was in 1999. It feels a little decadent to have someone on staff who makes fresh snacks and lunches! Connie Murphy was a student at the school and after she graduated high school, she came back here to work. She asked the board if she could create a hot lunch program. The building's kitchen was used for snack storage before she got here 3 years ago, and with her efforts it is now approved by the state as a catering kitchen. Connie does a great job and her food is delicious.

My secretary, Emily, is incredibly organized! All the files are up to date and there's nothing to worry about in terms of admin work. She's sharp as a tack.

The school contracts with a company, "A la Carte", to teach art and music to the three and four year olds. This idea of contracting out the teaching seems popular here. These lessons are called "specials." I don't love this idea because the specials cut into the children's free time. I'll watch how it works at this school and make a decision for next year.

I really like this group, Mom. Overall they are nice and most of them seem genuinely happy to meet me. I've got some big shoes to fill. The past director was well respected, and taught many of them what they know. I can imagine that this group is a little hesitant of change. It'll be okay. They don't know me yet, but I know they will be okay.

Love you Mom!

TO: ALL STAFF
FROM: DJ
DATE: AUGUST 25
RE: THANK YOU!

Hi everyone!

I hope you enjoyed our first 3 days together! I feel like we accomplished a great deal. Thank you all for the warm welcome you gave me last week.

Before we dive into the school year, let's recap what we covered during professional development. Our ice breaker in the garden yard was the introduction to a year of building relationships and community. I enjoyed hearing the stories of your families, and was glad to know that you also learned about each other.

We connected the research about how children learn with the importance of being intentional teachers. Some of what we discussed was new to you. During our discussion of the Vermont standards for kindergarten readiness, we noted that decoding (reading) and writing are not required skills for four year olds.

The amount of time used for teaching letters and sounds can now be used to offer free time experiences that increase their independence, i.e. getting dressed, communicating their needs, caring for each other, problem solving skills, etc. You can also use that time to bring interesting materials into the classroom for the children to study.

Remember when we practiced setting up materials in an intentional way? Jacquie and Jenn sorted rocks and put them in glass baby food jars. They displayed the jars on a mirror to offer visual appeal. Then they took a few big shells and placed some small rocks in one and larger rocks in the other. Next to the rocks, they placed a magnifying glass. They told us their intent was to encourage the children to explore and maybe sort the rocks by size. We all agreed that this display was much more interesting than the old bowl of rocks that was sitting in the science area.

Developmentally appropriate practice and child centered learning are proven to be excellent ways to teach children. This combination of the constructivist and sociocultural theories tells us to create experiences that allow children to construct meaning. Giving children time to have these experiences lets them share what they are learning with their peers. The role of teacher as facilitator means you "guide" learning experiences, not "teach knowledge."

I believe wholeheartedly in this approach. I've spent 25 years studying it and watching it work with children all around the country. I am so convinced that this works I'll put my position on the line. Take my suggestions seriously. If it does not show positive results, I will resign. Period. I mean it. This approach works and works well. I'm that certain.

Thank you again for the warm welcome. I'm looking forward to our first day on Monday!

DJ

MONDAY MEMO!

August 29

Good morning! It's our first official Monday Memo!

Today should flow smoothly (cross your fingers!). Because the Lambs are coming in tomorrow, Susan and Barb will be available all day today to help with anything you may need. The rest of you will be here only half day today and then tomorrow we begin a brand new year with a FULL house! Half day children will leave at 1:00 and the rest of the gang will either leave at 3:30 or stay till 6:00. You have your lists so you know who is doing what. If someone comes in who is not on your list, just give Emily a call in the office. She's the boss of the paperwork. (Yay Emily!)

There will be no specials this week, so enjoy the additional time with your children. And since the playground schedules are not yet posted, feel free to go outside whenever you and your class feel the need. So, with the new garden yard, the red yard, and the bike yard, you guys can all go outside at once and still be able to enjoy the space. Share and take turns!

The Parents Committee "Back to School" lunch will be delivered by 1:00. I think you all placed your orders, but if not, please tell Emily by 9:45. She has the list and is calling it in.

This week is about welcoming friends and building relationships. Don't get bogged down making projects. Take the time to get to know your children. Parents want to know that their little gifts from God will be happy and safe. Please keep that in mind as you talk to them. Emily created distribution lists for you with their emails. Grant, since you mentioned that you want to tweet this year, Emily added the parents' tweet names to your list.

We are closed Monday for Labor Day. We posted this on the windows of the front door; however, please add this info to any emails you send your parents this week. We want to reach the parents any way we can.

Thanks, everyone, for your energy and enthusiasm as we begin a new year together.

This will be a great year!
DJ

September 1

Hey Beth,

I got your letter. You sound like you are having a really good time getting to know your teachers. Keep it up! You are going to rock this school!

My first preschool started with 132 children and 25 staff, and with the addition one year later, grew to 234 kids and 49 teachers. I have such wonderful memories of those early years. All I can say is, "Thank God I refused to quit and had wonderful mentors who believed in me."

I devoted time to reading books about business, leadership, and sales. I learned valuable tools like managing without fear and increasing a company's bottom line. I learned about mission statements, great customer service, moving cheese, breaking boards, and eating fire. But I never found anything specific about running an excellent preschool or leading a team of teachers responsible for the good and welfare of our littlest citizens.

I developed a theory about managing teachers: Every teacher has her own unique style. Teachers whose methods differ from mine are not necessarily wrong. They are simply on a different stage of their journey. My job is to determine where each teacher is on his or her path and use that knowledge to help him or her grow.

Think about your philosophy for teaching children. You believe that children need to think on their own. You want them to represent their own thoughts. You push for small group learning with the children so they can each be heard and practice being collaborative. You want children to have opportunities to learn the answers on their own so you encourage reflective thinking practices.

Now think about your philosophy for teaching **teachers**. Some items are non-negotiable: everyone has to be on the same page in terms of understanding how children learn, health and safety practices, and DAP. However, you may have a teacher who loves science and shares that passion with the children. Wonderful! Celebrate that! Your job is to make sure the teachers understand and follow the non-negotiables and help them grow as individuals. Just like we observe children to understand how they learn, you have to observe your teachers to understand how they teach. The question is: **what are you looking for when you observe your teachers and what do you do about what you see?** We can talk later about what to do about it, but for now this what you are looking for:

- How does she relate to the children in terms of verbal and non-verbal communication? Does she show respect?

- How does he plan for the children's learning? Are his methods developmentally appropriate?

- How fully does she use the environment as a teaching tool?

- How does he communicate with families about the classroom activities?

- How does he work with his fellow teachers?

- What kinds of professional development does she look for? What does she like to learn?

Start there. Get to know your staff. Remember: It's all about building relationships. Can you build them? Yes, you can!

TO: JENNIFER
FROM: DJ
DATE: SEPTEMBER 2
RE: PHOTOS _fa authentic assessment_

Dear Jennifer,

Thank you for sharing your photos with me today! I am so excited to see such great moments captured from your class. The photo of Joey with his little tongue hanging out as he tried to figure out where to put the block just cracked me up!

You have an eye for authentic assessment. Your photos of the children engaged in activities tell me that you grasp how they learn. This is a key factor of developmentally appropriate practice because once you realize that learning happens while the children are playing, you are able to intentionally create experiences that are achievable and challenging.

I encourage you to stop taking photos of single incidents, but rather seek to shoot a series of photos, perhaps 4 or 5 at a time, so we can see how the children approach their work. Do it over the course of a few weeks. Once you have a little collection, we can chat about both the experience of taking photos and the photos themselves.

Thanks!
DJ

TO: SUSAN
FROM: DJ
DATE: SEPTEMBER 6
RE: LICENSING – *Communicating w/ Parents*

Dear Susan,

This is a follow up from our conversation this afternoon. Whenever we chat about the important stuff (and that means things that are important to either you or me), I usually follow up with a letter, so we are both clear on what happened and what we decided to do.

Today was pretty hectic for us since both the health department and childcare licensing showed up at the same time. That has never happened to me before and I want to make sure that never happens again.

When parents pick up their children, they look forward to hearing something positive about their child's day.

What you said to Maricel's mom was neither positive nor necessary. I understand the children were all eating macaroni and cheese for lunch and that sometimes the kids pick up the food from the floor, but to tell a parent that her child ate her lunch from off the floor is not comforting. She sees it as horrifying, which is why both agencies showed up, and why Maricel is no longer coming here.

Since your two year olds are adorable, finding something to share about each child should be pretty easy. Use the notebooks we gave you to keep a record of the stories.

Remember that parents rely on you to create the picture of their child's day. The stories you share are what they carry with them when they are separated from their children. Your message must be appropriate and positive. If you are unsure of what to share with parents, ask me or Barb.

Thanks.
DJ

Dear Mom,

This letter is being titled "The Good, the Bad and the Ugly."

The Good: The Monkeys class (three year olds) spent the better part of last week playing with glue! Debra let them shake and pour and cajole the glue out of the bottles just to watch it all drip down. There was glue on the table, in a few heads of hair, under shoes... it was wonderful. The children learned first-hand how to squeeze the bottle and how glue feels when it dries on their hands. I tried to show them how to make fingernails out of the dried glue (remember when Cheryl and I would do that for hours at a time?). No one would do it! I'll try it again another time.

The Lions class (three year olds) have been getting lots more time to play! Jennifer jumped at the chance to offer extended play time and has been taking wonderful photos of the children and their discoveries. My favorite so far is one of a little girl who realized that yellow and blue made green! This class is definitely on the right path to DAP!

The Bad: In my Lambs class (two year olds) I have a teacher (Susan) who really shouldn't be here. She loves to bake and I guess she loves her job, but she has no technical skills when it comes to teaching young children. She is confused as to why children cannot share or won't sit for circle time. She put a child in time out this morning for not listening. We don't put children in time out for not listening, Mom. We don't put children in time out, period! I have so much to teach her.

The Ugly: My Bears class (four year olds) reminds me of prison. (OK, that was harsh, but it's just not fun in there.) Deirdre, the teacher, has a checklist of what every five year old is expected to know and "tests" them during the day. They have "table work" for 45 minutes every morning. You know what "table work" is? Letter of the week pages, color sheets and a journal entry! 15 minutes for each one! AND, after the "table work" time, the children have circle time where they go over the days of the week, state capitals, and telling time. Yep, telling time. THEY ARE FOUR, Mom! They spend the first hour and a half of their day doing lessons designed for First Graders. I can't believe this is considered acceptable. And to top it off, they are expected to behave themselves!

Mom, I sat at the table where the children were doing a worksheet on the letter A. They were told to trace the letter with their finger, copy the letter 10 times, then color the pictures of the airplane, apple and aardvark! I decided to do the sheet with them. After 4, maybe 5 minutes all of the children were finished. They were told to wait for 10 more minutes before they could move to the next table. Looking for something to do, we started talking to each other. The table talk was about someone's grandmother coming in for the weekend and having to go to the hospital. I was fascinated by their discussion until the point when the teacher announced that we needed to be quiet so the others can think.

This is not going to work for me.

This is going to be one crazy year. At this moment I can honestly say I may have bitten off more than I can chew, but I'm not going to quit. I believe in this. There is a part of me that knows I can make this an amazing developmentally appropriate school, even if I have to fire them all and start from scratch! I think my first step will be to calm down. Then I'll start a priority list. Think good thoughts!

Love you Mom!

A Note from DJ

September 6

Dear Beth,

Hi there friend! How's it going at your school? Are you still building relationships? Getting to know the troops? That's all I am doing over here, too!

After I was hired, people were talking about the new director and how she ruled with an iron fist! Ha! Me?! I'm just a visionary that wants to create the best possible school. I'm in no way the autocrat that was their last director. (Between you and me, it seems to me like these teachers were kept on a very short leash.) Here are some examples:

The classrooms are set up almost identically. Each room has perfectly matching tables and chairs, and is painted exactly alike. I noticed this when I first started, but I thought the teachers would use their own styles to set up their room for the school year. There is simply no ownership in the rooms, either by the children or the teachers. There are virtually no photos of the children displayed anywhere, and most of the rooms have identical store bought wall decorations. (Alphabet, colors, shapes and number posters.)

Even though I explained developmentally appropriate practice and the value of free play during professional development, most of the teachers act like they don't understand why I asked them to extend the length of center play. They use this time as a mini break for themselves, prepping materials or cleaning. Only one class is using the time to observe children.

I'm going to spend time with the teachers in their classes during center time to role model the value of play. I'll point out what the children are doing and how that relates to the domains of learning. It won't take long before the children show evidence of math, science, and other cognitive skills, and I'll show the teachers how to ask questions to guide the children to higher level problem solving. I'll also use this time to point out how language and literacy occurs naturally through play.

This staff needs to take ownership for their classroom and its daily schedule. I am going to eliminate their playground schedule. They have 3 play yards and 5 classrooms! Why would you need a schedule? Go out when you need to, just find an open yard! My approach to making this change is a little indirect. I told them I "forgot" to make a playground schedule, (which is true because once I decided not to have one I forgot all about it). I told them to go out as they saw fit. Maybe this can be the beginning of empowering the teachers to believe in themselves and their children.

Keep me posted about your school. I want to know what's going on over there. Have you drafted your plan? What's first on your list? As much as you want to wave a magic wand over that building, you can't change everyone at the same time. Create a list of teachers who are interested in learning and have the skills to make a change. Then work with one teacher at a time as you continue to share your vision with the rest of the team. Before you know it you will have a small group of believers that will grow in time. It really works!

Week two is around the corner!

DJ

MONDAY MEMO!

(MONDAY MEMO on a TUESDAY!)
Tuesday, September 6

Welcome to week 2!

Jacquie and Jennifer took a bunch of great photos last week! Keep it up! Emily sent you the pictures to start an all-staff discussion about using photos. In the past you used photos to showcase a child holding his project. I'd like to see what other options we have for using photography in the classroom. We created a writing area on the staff bathroom wall and added some Sharpies to jot down thoughts or comments. Please use this to share ideas.

The Tiger room adopted a guinea pig! James' mother works at PetPlace and brought it in for the school. They haven't named him yet, but as soon as they do, Mrs. W. and her children are planning on having a little naming ceremony. We'll keep you posted.

Sorry about the playground schedule. I saw that you guys are doing pretty well without one. How do you think it's going? Do we really need a schedule? Unless I hear differently from you, I am going to keep the playground schedule open for you to determine when to go out.

Thank you for accepting the challenge of allowing the children extra time to explore and play on their own. When children play, they are problem solving, using their imaginations, and practicing social skills like sharing and negotiating. Sometimes they lead and other times they learn to follow. When they are given 45 minutes or longer to play, their block structures become more intricate, their dramatic play stories become more involved, and even their art looks different. Children need time to play, reflect (think about) what they just did, develop new strategies, and continue to play. Extending their time from 20 minutes to 45 gives them the opportunity they need to take their learning to a deeper level.

Do you remember during professional development when I gave you paper and tape to make sculptures? Many of you, thinking you had only a few minutes, created something quickly. When you learned you had 20 minutes, you took the time to reflect on your sculptures and make them more creative and beautiful. Some of you said that you wanted even more time to see what else you could create. That is what we offer the children when we extend free play/center time. We give them the opportunity to reflect on their work and deepen their learning.

While the children are in their centers, sit near them and listen to them. Be a fly on the wall and let them talk. Don't lead the conversation. Just listen to them. Ask clarifying questions. In time you will see patterns emerge and become aware of their interests.

A good rule of thumb is to offer free play/centers for at least one third of the time they are at school. Since most of the children are here for 4 hours, that means we should offer them at least 1 hour and 20 minutes of center time. We will use this time to observe and get to know the children better.

When you look at your classroom's current schedule, you'll see that the children spend a great deal of time in large group activities: circle time, specials, group snack projects, lunch and nap, but less than 1 hour of center time. As we discussed during professional development, this leaves very little time for the children to explore and play on their own. We will increase their free play opportunities to at least 1½ hours a day by winter break.

In the past I've seen teachers extend free time by opening a snack center rather than having a whole group snack time. This can easily give the children an additional 30 minutes since they will no longer need to wait for the others to wash their hands before they can eat. Another easy way to allow for more free time is to eliminate the whole group project/learning experience, and work with the children in small groups during center time. Ideally, all morning will be open free play, with a small meeting at the beginning of the day. This will happen as you realize that children's play (supported by you) is how they learn. I'll come into your rooms and discuss how to make this work in your class.

Does anyone want an aquarium? Let me know!

P.S. Sometimes my inspiration comes to me in the form of a song. I wrote this for us since we are all just beginning together.

(ahem)

I've Only Just Begun

(To be sung to the tune of "We've Only Just Begun" by The Carpenters)

I've only just begun, to learn...

Seeing my friends again...a kiss from Mom and I'm on my way. (I've only begun)

Before the meeting time.... I play...

Building with wooden blocks, reading books and pounding clay.

(And yet I've just begun)

Sharing my food is not what I should do...sometimes I toss it in the air...it flies.

Eating a piece or two that's on the floor, don't think my mom would really care.

And then when nap time comes.....I cry....

Holding my beddy bear, I find a place and I rest my head...

(You see, I've just begun)

Sharing my toys seems rather new to me...I want to grab your doll away ... oh my.

(Oh my),

Talking about it only frustrates us, but we can learn along the way..... Together, together...

And when I get picked up, I smile....can't wait to come again...

I've got a plan and might bite my friend....

And yet I've just begun.

September 7

Hey Mom,

I made a friend today! He's 4 years old and stole my heart in under 2 minutes. I walked into the building and he ran up to me and put up his hand as if to stop me. Then he announced:

I don't know who you are! Whose mom are you?

Me: My sons are Dan and Nick. But they don't come here. My name is Miss DJ and I am the preschool director. What is your name?

Him: (In a sing song manner) My name is William. William Hackett. W-I-double L-I-A-M, H-A-C-K-E- double T. William Hackett, rhymes with bracket.

Me: William Hackett, it's very nice to meet you.

William: I know. I am adorable.

And then he ran off.

Best encounter of the day. Unfortunately after that, I walked into the Lion's room just in time to see Jacquie reprimand a child. I could tell when I walked in that she knew she had behaved inappropriately because she immediately changed her tone from anger and frustration to a sugar sweet singsong voice. "Hi Miss DJ, we were just discussing how to be a friend. Katie was having a problem remembering that hands are for loving, not hurting, right, Katie?"

To tell you I was upset would be a gross understatement. You know me. Very little makes me upset, but treating children with disrespect is by far the worst. I looked at Katie and saw such a sad face. Her big beautiful eyes were filling with tears and her bottom lip was trembling. I didn't want to blow up in front of the children, so I asked Katie to take a walk with me. She took my hand and we spent a few minutes walking in silence while we both calmed down. We went outside, looked at trees, and talked about the birds. When she looked ready, I asked her if she wanted to talk about what happened in the classroom. She shook her head no. I asked if she felt ready to go back and she asked me if I would play with her. When I told her I had to go back into my office, she started crying and told me that no one wanted to play with her. (I needed to know that - now we have something to work on!)

I asked her what she liked to do in the classroom. She told me that Brenda liked to paint and she liked to stir the colors. We decided to go back in the classroom to see if anyone wanted to mix colors with her. When we went into the room, Jacquie was standing near the door ready to say something to Katie. I put up my hand to stop her and announced to the class that Katie was planning on going to the art center to mix some paint colors and did anyone what to join her? Immediately, two children ran to the art center.

At lunch I spoke with Jacquie. She told me she thought that Katie was wrong to hit someone and explained that Katie had behaved hurtfully these last few days - yada yada yada. I asked her if she knew that Katie felt sad that no one would play with her. Jacquie said she knew Katie was sad and didn't know what to do and since Katie cries all the time, she thought it was more like just whining.

At that moment I thought to myself "This woman really doesn't understand DAP." I explained that at this age children have a wide range of emotions and can feel very strongly about what may seem to us to be tiny. I asked her what she might have done if she had believed Katie was truly sad and needed support. She told me that she would help her find a way to play with someone, or help her find something she liked to do on her own. I asked if helping Katie might have avoided the frustration that led to hitting Jonah. Jacquie thought maybe it could have helped.

I told Jacquie that as teachers we are powerful. We can use our power over, for, or with the children. In this case, Jacquie could have used her power FOR Katie, helping her work through her frustration. Instead she chose to use her power OVER Katie, physically restraining her and demanding her attention. Jacquie looked thoughtful and said she understood. She said she felt really bad about ignoring Katie. In the past, she told me, the last director would tell the children that if they don't use their words, the teachers can't help. Jacquie said she really didn't know what to teach the children to say when they were upset. She told me she would try to be more aware of their feelings.

In time I believe she will understand her role differently – as a partner with the children. If not, I will have a decision to make. No one has the right to use their power over children like that.

I was very lucky to have you as a mom. You and Dad always treated me with respect. Sure you got mad, but you never made me feel insignificant and powerless.

Love you!

DJ

Hi Jacquie,

As we discussed yesterday, your exchange with Katie was uncomfortable and disconcerting. What I saw when I entered the room was you, holding Katie's hand, speaking loudly at her to stop hitting. It was only when you saw me that your behavior changed and you announced to me that she was having a problem "using her hands for loving, not hurting." Katie was on the edge of tears when I walked with her out of the classroom.

Northern Lights Preschool has a reputation of being a loving, nurturing and safe place for children. Reprimanding children with loud voices and arm grabbing is neither loving nor safe. Regardless of how Katie behaved this past week, there is never a behavior that calls for yelling, berating, or humiliation.

Katie told me that no one wants to play with her. When you told me that you were aware of that, but thought it was because she was behaving meanly, you indicated to me that you, too, felt she was unworthy of love or friendship. That is not how we help children learn social skills or give them a sense of belonging.

Katie needed someone to take the time to understand why she was sad, and guide her to make appropriate choices. You are the one hired to do this. It saddens me that you failed to meet that responsibility.

In times like this, first and foremost, you must see each child as a confident and loving soul who is trying to figure out the delicate politics of social skills and negotiation. Behaviors like hitting, yelling, and throwing toys are the only way they know to communicate their feelings. Being punished for sharing how they feel is wrong.

As teachers we are responsible for our children's development in not only cognitive learning, but also emotional and social growth. We are responsible for identifying what causes them frustration. We are responsible for being compassionate and patient. We are the ones responsible for guiding them towards new choices and new ways to communicate. When we pass judgment on a child by reprimanding or humiliating them, or worse, ignore that which frustrates them, we lose the position of supporter, and can no longer offer emotional help. And when that happens, we are no longer effective teachers.

Remember the concept of Absolute Intentional Regard. Even if a child hits others, we see him as someone who is trying to communicate and we are the ones who need to figure out his message.

Teachers who practice AIR have a default setting in their internal talk that is different from other teachers. For example, when a child cries at drop off, almost every teacher will rush to soothe him. After a few weeks, however, many teachers become less responsive, assuming "that's just the way he is, he's a crier." After a month, those teachers might even begin to put him in a time out spot, alleging that his tears are upsetting the other children.

A teacher who practices AIR will continue to try everything possible to help this child, be it one week or one month into the process. Her self-talk is always, "How can I help guide this child through this transition?" rather than "Why does he cry so much? He just doesn't belong here. I don't have the time for this." The first statement reflects an attitude that this child will succeed, while the second has already decided he is going to fail.

In looking at the behaviors of your children, please begin giving them some AIR. Give them the benefit of the doubt. Yes, they are crying, biting, and hitting, but more importantly, they are trying to tell you something. What is it? Ask them. Are you sad? Do you miss Mommy? Did something happen? Do you need help? Offer unconditional support. The children will begin to trust that you have their best interest at heart and they will come to you on their own for help.

Because of today's situation, it may take a little while for Katie to feel safe coming around you. That's not how we want our children to feel.

We discussed using phrases like "We are all learning, that's why we are in school", and "Would you like a do-over? We can try to talk to Sarah another way", or "Can you clarify what you mean? I can help you tell Sarah what you would like." Guiding young children through social situations is one of the most important things you can do as a teacher. Learning colors and numbers means nothing if they cannot communicate their needs in an appropriate way.

I realize this is new information for you. I want you to focus on your relationships with the children over the next few weeks. Take the time to understand what they are trying to communicate. I will be coming into your class often to help; however, feel free to come to me anytime.

Thank you.
DJ

Hi everyone!

Like we covered in training, DAP entails teaching to the individual child, not the whole group. It means that what we do is aligned with where children are developmentally, not where we "expect" them to be.

Over the last few days I have had a chance to go into all of your classrooms. During those visits, I've noticed several instances of children getting in trouble over arbitrary rules. There appears to be a rule in this school that children must be quiet and give the teacher their full attention when she/he is speaking. It is presented as a rule (or game) called "crisscross applesauce, eyes on teacher." The problem with the game is that not all children are able to play, because this expectation is inappropriate for three and four year olds.

From this point on, I want you to stop putting adult motivation behind children's behaviors. When you do, you put unnecessary stress on both of you. They are children. They haven't had all the experiences you've had so their behaviors come from the limited encounters they've had so far. When you see them misbehave, it's because they are trying to communicate something. Preschool children are not expected to behave as adults. They are unable to control many of their impulses and are not equipped with the tools to focus on something that is not interesting. When you expect/request/create a game about a behavior that they are unable to deliver, you send the message that they are bad listeners who need to be fixed. That is simply not true.

Children want to connect what you are saying with what they already know. When you teach something for which they have no previous experience, some children may appear uninterested. That is because if they cannot make a connection while listening to you, they will do whatever they can to make a connection on their own. In other words, if you want the children to really be interested in what you have to say, change how you say it.

Please come to me with any questions. Thanks.

DJ

Deirdre: Hi DJ. I understand what you are saying in the staff memo. I don't have a problem with this but my challenge is the parents. They want their children to sit quietly during circle time and practice counting. They want their children to come home with worksheets so they can share what they learned about letters. They know that their child is expected to be quiet and learn. They see us as a school and that's what we do here. I know what you are saying about letting them learn individually, but I don't think the parents will be happy knowing that their child only got a part of the lessons, not all of them. Our parents have pretty high expectations here. It may be a little different from your old school in Las Vegas. I just thought you might want to know.

DJ: Thanks for sharing your thoughts. I have explained DAP to hundreds of parents over the years and without exception they all wanted it for their child. Developmentally appropriate practice recognizes each child as an individual and helps them learn at their own pace. It makes total sense and is nothing to be ashamed of. Offering children letter worksheets is not appropriate because while it is achievable, it is in no way challenging. Expecting children to count by 5s is not appropriate because, at their age, it is challenging, but not yet achievable.

Deirdre: I am not worried about the children. They are wonderful and so smart. I am sure all of them will succeed. They are deep thinkers. Yesterday William told me he thought he could see the stars during the daytime. He squinted his eyes and told me that it helps. He's so adorable.

DJ: Did you create an experience that caused William to look for stars in the daytime? Where did that come from? And what did you say to him?

Deirdre: I didn't do anything. He just told me. I told him what a smart boy he was and that he might be a doctor or a scientist one day. Then he went on to play with the others.

DJ: When a child comes to you with a story, idea, or new thought, he is probably interested in learning more about it. Your job is to find out what interests him. Observations are the key to becoming developmentally appropriate. Do you think William decided to squint his eyes outside to see the stars only today, or is this ongoing? Do you think he might have an interest in the stars and the sky? Or maybe an interest in what his eyes can do? There is value in taking the time to determine what interests him.

Deirdre: This is confusing. None of the other children are interested in the seeing stars during the day. Am I supposed to do something only for William? Are you asking me to tailor every activity for every child? That seems unreasonable, DJ. I have 16 children. Are you asking me to come up with 16 different activities for every child every day?

DJ: No, Deirdre. At any given time you may have 3 or 4 different experiences going on in the classroom. Four year olds have similar interests and similar abilities. By taking a cue from William and offering binoculars and bringing in materials to make telescopes and other tools, you will inspire others to embrace this interest. I don't want you to change everything you do. I'm saying look at your practice and replace inappropriate experiences with ones that are exciting, challenging and achievable.   Let's make time to sit down and chat about this.

A Note from DJ

September 10

Hey Beth,

I'm getting to know the staff slowly but surely. There's potential here; I can feel it. A few of them are listening to my suggestions and actually considering what I am saying.

I have a fours teacher (Deirdre) who needs some work. She needs a dose of anti-denial medication. Can I buy that on Amazon? Seriously, this woman looks me in the eye and tells me that she is developmentally appropriate, yet gives her children worksheets every morning. She'll come around. I believe she will. I just have to get her to understand she can't opt out of being developmentally appropriate.

Thankfully she has Grant, who is hands down one of the kindest teachers I have ever met. He is funny and has such a high level of respect for the children. Right now he is stuck in her shadow since she is the lead teacher. (Here the leads pretty much rule the roost and the assistants don't have much say in curriculum planning.) Grant won't be an assistant for long. One day he will make a wonderful lead teacher.

I love my Lions teachers! (The Lions are one of the three year old classes.) Even though I have to work with Jacquie on classroom management skills, she is committed and determined to learn. She is interested in doing what is right, but she just isn't sure what "right" is. Her co-teacher Jennifer is wonderful but doesn't like conflict, so she never corrected Jacquie's teaching style. Jacquie's ready to learn. I can teach her.

On a different note, I gave them the camera that the parents committee donated and asked them to photo-journal their classroom. It was the best thing I ever did. They are taking this seriously and their enthusiasm is contagious. These teachers are learning about assessment and don't even know it!

DJ

Jacquie: Thank you for helping me with Katie last week. You were right. I was so embarrassed because you saw me talking to her. I really didn't know what else to do. I will try to understand the children's behaviors differently so I can help them. I like that AIR thing. I want to be someone with AIR.

DJ: No worries. You're on the right path. Being aware of your actions is a start. Spend time understanding your children and modeling respect. The rest will work out. By the way, I think you are someone who understands Absolute Intentional Regard (AIR). I've seen you speak to parents in a non-judgmental way. You always find the good in people. What you need to do now is realize that the behaviors you see from the children are indicators of how they feel, not who they are.

DJ: Hi Grant! It was great to see you watch the children during center time. It looked like you were observing their play to determine their interests with the phones. If you want to discuss your observations, I'd be glad to spend time chatting with you.

Grant: I've been watching these kids tweet each other ever since school started. They fight over the cell phones, (You wouldn't happen to have a few more lying around would you - LOL?) They send messages and tweets to each other! Once they send a message, they give the phone to their friend to "read" what they wrote. It is hilarious! You can hear them as they talk about the messages they are sending. Toby sent "I am Batman!" Haha!

DJ: I love this! You may have found an interest that can be developed. Do you know how you might scaffold their learning? (Other than with more phones?) Remember that developmentally appropriate activities are both challenging and achievable. Don't offer anything too easy. Think about it and let's chat more later.

MONDAY MEMO!

September 12

Hello Friends! Remember those charts that were in my office? I combined them to generate a list of what we value at Northern Lights Preschool.

- We value a culture of respect, collaboration, and community.

- We value the relationship between teachers and parents.

- We believe that children are naturally curious and seek connections in everything around them.

- We believe that real learning begins with the joy of play and discovery.

- We believe that children are natural investigators and the learning environment should reflect that belief.

- We believe in giving the children opportunities to see themselves as part of a larger community, with both rights and responsibilities.

- We believe that teachers are co-learners who support children's natural curiosity, who ask questions, scaffold learning, and record progress with stories and photos.

- We value ongoing professional development for teachers and opportunities to support parents on their journey of parenthood.

Did I miss something? Please let me know if you think there needs to be something added or deleted. After we agree about this, I will make a poster that contains this mission and we will all sign in agreement.

In other news:

Mrs. W. and her Tigers seemed to have a pretty good experience with the "What do we call our pet?" campaign. I have to say, it was very exciting to see the children with their clipboards and pencils in hand, stopping parents in the hall saying, "Please pick a name for our new pig... Zizzy, Franklin or Squish." Very cool!

Mrs. W. shared with me that she is going to retire at the end of this school year. She and her husband are moving to Tucson to be with her new granddaughter. Congratulations! We are very happy for you. (And really sad for us.) :(

The Bears class is incredibly interested in "tweeting". They want to tweet each other "for real" (as opposed to maybe pretending with a phone) so Grant is working on a way to make that happen. What a great way to bring literacy into the classroom. Mom and Dad tweet, so why not them? Do you have any ideas for them? Feel free to share your thoughts on the board in the the bathroom or you can tweet Grant @ missergrant, since that is what the children call him.

A few reminders:

The "A la Carte" people are out this week, so no art or music classes. HOWEVER, I know that you know that I know that YOU know some great art experiences you can offer your children. Why not add glitter to a bowl of finger-paint? Or add paint to a spray bottle so they can spray a masterpiece? Have you thought about just offering them a few permanent markers and fabric? After they are finished you can show them how to use a dropper to drip some rubbing alcohol onto the fabric and the colors will run, kinda like tie-dye. There you go! Three things to try in place of the a la Carte folks!

For Wednesday's lunch, Connie will bring the tortillas, beans, and cheese to your rooms. If the children want to help prepare them, (this is an optional center, not a required activity – we are not abusing child labor laws here!) watch them wash their hands thoroughly and make sure they wear food prep gloves. No one is worried about the look of the burritos, but Connie's hoping for a 3:1 bean:cheese ratio.

Staff meeting next week! 5:30 Thursday, September 22. Pot luck (you can bring it in the morning and Connie will heat it up for us) and since we are all well over 21, I will bring in some wine. Not whine: wine!

Have a great week!

Northern Lights Preschool

318 North Harbor Grove
Burlington, VT 05401
555-912-1987
dj@northern-lights-preschool.com

September 13

Dear Mrs. Walker,

It was great speaking with you this morning. Of course we still have a place for Maricel in Susan's class! We love her and can't wait to welcome her and you back with open arms. I am crediting your account for last week's tuition.

I appreciate that you shared your concerns about what happened last week. Susan is an incredibly kind and loving teacher and she is always looking for opportunities to grow. Your feedback concerning her communication has already been valuable in coaching her. Thank you for bringing to my attention that she told the parents that some of the children were "a little bit wild" and that they needed a time out, but "we don't do time out over here." It's true that we don't use time out because we have a better way that empowers children to succeed in social situations.

We model the behaviors we want our children to learn. This helps them see appropriate responses they can try when they are frustrated or angry.

When we see that a young child is in a socially challenging situation, the teacher will let him try to work it out then step in to offer help. If a child is doing something that can hurt herself or the others, we do not isolate the child, rather, the teacher stays with her until she is calmer and able to rejoin the group. Normally this only takes a few minutes. We want to offer Maricel and her friends the best opportunity to become socially competent and caring people. If you have any questions at all, feel free to speak with me.

Again, I am so glad that your family's coming back to join ours!

All the best,

DJ

Hi Mom,

Today I got tickled watching my friend William Hackett in action. Poor thing is in Deirdre's class and doesn't quite fit her criteria for the perfect student. Deirdre's lesson was one to one counting up to the number 4. First of all, William IS four. He knows 4. Teaching him how to count to four is not considered cool. Nor is it developmentally appropriate. Check this out.

This school currently uses the worksheet method of teaching. The teachers show an apple to the group and say, "This is an apple, everyone say apple. Apple starts with A. Everyone say A. Now let's glue 4 apple seeds onto our paper."

Busy children are happy children. Apparently Deirdre never got that memo. She expected the children to sit and hold their seeds while she counted them out; one child at a time. I almost groaned out loud at the impending boredom.

William caught on to her plan rather quickly and decided to count out his seeds by himself. He called out, "I have four seeds, too!" The teacher just smiled and waved at him to wait a few minutes. Not a good idea, teacher. William got bored waiting. (Can you blame him?) I glanced over just in time to see him place an apple seed on his middle finger and fling it at another child. I had to look away so no one would see me smiling.

What happened next was a cluster of crazy.

Deirdre stopped her counting, walked over to William, and asked him what he did and why. William is no dummy. He looked down and said, "It fell." The other children had to wait and watch as little William got reprimanded for flinging seeds and then lying about it. If that wasn't awkward enough, Alan got bored and put a seed up his nose, then Ashley ate a seed which made Octavia cry because now "Ashley is going to die because an apple tree is going to grow in her belly." Then Arthur tried to take a seed from Daniel because he is going to be five next month and should have 5 seeds not four. And where was Deirdre? Talking to William; explaining why lying (a common behavior for four year olds) was wrong.

On one hand, it was hilarious. On the other, it made me want to cry.

Deirdre is definitely a teacher who needs some work. I plan to spend time with her, modeling DAP, scaffolding, and teaching AIR. She needs to change her ways and I hope she comes on board soon. I believe in this and I hope she will, too! (It's a no brainer really: put numbers into the wells of an egg carton and challenge the children to a seed counting game. Same one to one correspondence, different approach, no seed flinging.)

Although, like I taught you when I was 6, nothing can guarantee that a child won't try to shove a seed up her nose. How was I to know it would take a visit to the ER to get that seed out? Noses are like magnets for tiny round things.

On a different note, I spoke with Cheryl this afternoon. I can't believe it's back. Why can't she get a break from all of this? After all those surgeries, chemo treatments, and radiation, we were so hopeful that it was gone for good. We were told that all she had to do was make it three years without recurrence and she would be out of danger. She's one month away from her three year anniversary. It's so unfair.

After we spoke, I went into the garden yard and cried. I cried for what she is going to have to endure again. I cried for all of us who are hurting right along with her. This will be her biggest fight to date and I pray she wins.

Love you Mom. I miss you.

Northern Lights Preschool

318 North Harbor Grove
Burlington, VT 05401
555-912-1987
dj@northern-lights-preschool.com

September 16

Dear Mrs. Hackett,

I've got a little story to tell you about your savvy son William. I went into his classroom today and he told me I needed a haircut. Mr. Grant and some children had been exploring their new interest in hair salons, so I went along with it and asked him if he knew of any good hairdressers. He took my hand and brought me to the dramatic play area where he told me to sit down. Once there, he said, "5 dollars, please." The rest of our chat went like this:

Me: Five dollars! That's a great price. Maybe I should get my hair colored, too? How much is that?
William: Color too costs 8 dollars.
Me: So, how much will I have to pay you?
William: 8 dollars, but you have to pay now. After you pay I can cut your hairs.
Me: Oh, I have to pay in advance? Before you cut my hair? That's uncommon.
William: Yes. 8 dollars now, please. First you pay. Then I cut your hair.
Me: OK, here is the money. (We high five) I would like a cut and blow dry also, please.
William: (Walks away)
Me: Hey wait! Aren't you going to cut my hair?
William: No, thank you!
Me: But my hair...
William: (Sporting that big grin of his) Bye!

I think we are becoming fast friends.

Have a wonderful day!

MONDAY MEMO!

September 19

Hi Everyone,

Over the past 25 years, as I studied best practices in early childhood education, the vision of an excellent program was churning in my head. My goal is to bring that vision here.

My vision is a school where the teachers, children, and families learn together. It is a community based on mutual respect, joy, and wonder. Parents and teachers will see the children as competent members of the community and consider their ideas as seriously as they would their own. Teachers will use DAP to challenge the children to reach new and achievable goals. The children will feel safe to express themselves and take risks. The classrooms will burst with energy and excitement as children and teachers work together. That's the school I want. That's what the board agreed to and what has been proven to be excellence in early childhood education. Here is my rationale:

- Children who feel safe and validated don't spend their days looking for attention or control. That means teachers won't spend their day reprimanding children!

- Learning will be fun because children will feel like the teachers are their partners.

- When the children are engaged in work that they love, they will organically meet academic goals. By understanding this, our teachers will have less pressure to test skills and more time to enjoy their children.

- When teachers realize the children are learning, they will help the parents see that this approach produces positive social, academic, and emotional outcomes.

It's a beautiful thing. It will take time and is challenging in the beginning, but I promise you it is worth the effort.

Have a great week!

MONDAY MEMO!

September 26

The guinea pig has a name! If there was a rodent phonebook he could now have a listing. Please welcome (wait for it...) Zizzy to the Tigers' class! We had a great little naming celebration for Zizzy on Friday afternoon. Thanks, Susan, for bringing in all those great guinea pig shaped cookies. How cute! Jennifer took lots of photos and we put a little scrapbook page on the wall near the bathroom.

The process of naming Zizzy is an excellent example of developmentally appropriate practice. The teachers had discussions about names, let the children determine how they were going to decide the best name, encouraged on-street (in hallway) interviews with clipboards, and then created a presentation of the naming certificate along with some of the children's versions of their own birth certificates. Every step included something that interested the children.

Be aware that not EVERY child in Mrs. W.'s class participated in every activity during this experience. By giving the children a chance to work on what interested them, the teachers were better able to get to know each child and understand a little more about their learning styles. Some loved the creative process of name selection, others liked the social aspect of interviewing, and the artists loved creating certificates. Each child participated in the process and each child's contribution was valuable.

I noticed that some of you have also had experiences with child-led learning in your classrooms. Jacquie and Jenn took Grant's advice and now they download the morning's photos during naptime. When the children wake up, they check out the photos on the class computer. Jenn said that the children who work in the block center love it. They go to the computer looking for the updated photos and talk about what they made. I love to see that the children reflect on their work and plan their next steps. By reflecting and thinking about their work, the children are making new connections and becoming constructively engaged. In other words, the children are using their free time to play and learn. That's what I'm working towards.

Don't be afraid to try new things in your class. Watch the children play, ask yourself what interests them, then spend time looking for the answers. Try out an idea. Some will work, others won't. It's okay either way. What is important here is that you watched them, reflected on your observation, and then tried something new. Cool things will happen. I promise.

Hi guys!

My sister, Cheryl, is coming to town this weekend! She is the most wonderful sister in the world and such a great person to know! You are going to love her!   She gets in tonight and will come to school tomorrow. We plan to visit the classrooms in the morning. Cheryl loves children and I am willing to bet she'll make them animal balloons.

Also, I am ordering lunch from Delia's for everyone. You are all invited. We will have a picnic in the garden so leave your lunch money at home tomorrow!

Have a great afternoon!

DJ

TO: JACQUIE
FROM: DJ
DATE: SEPTEMBER 27
RE: FOLLOW UP ON AIR AND TOBIAS

Hi Jacquie,

It's been a few weeks and I wanted to follow up on our discussion about giving children Absolute Intentional Regard (AIR).

Jenn shared with me about the disagreement between Tobias and Brandon over the blocks. When she told me that you asked Tobias if it surprised him that the structure fell down, I said a little silent cheer for you. "Go Jacquie! Giving the benefit of the doubt to the child!" Of course Tobias' response didn't help the matter. But at least he was honest when he said he knew it would fall down and that he wanted Brandon to cry.

Tobias is very smart. He is aware of his actions and knows that his behavior can affect others. What you want to work on is WHY he chose to make Brandon cry. Was he bored? Is he upset about something? I don't believe that Tobias has a bad soul and wants to cause problems everywhere he goes. I think he wants to be a part of the action and is unsure how to make that happen. Please work with him to find his place in the classroom.

The practice of giving children Absolute Intentional Regard takes time and I'm very pleased to hear that you are working on it every day. Please don't hesitate to talk to me. It's not a sign of weakness to ask for help. It's a sign of strength. I'm here for you!

Thanks!
DJ

TO: SUSAN
FROM: DJ
DATE: SEPTEMBER 28
RE: MRS. MALONE

Hi Susan,

First of all, thanks for the macaroons. They were delicious.

Second, let's recap what we discussed this afternoon.

We rely on open communication with the families. Listening to them, responding to their needs, and offering help when possible; this is what we do. Mutual respect and trust builds partnerships, and we want partnerships. That is why trust is so important.

Mrs. Malone shared with you, in confidence, that she and her husband were having problems and were considering divorce. This is incredibly private information and should be kept that way. By telling other parents, you broke her trust. We want to help the Malone family during this stressful time, but if Mom doesn't trust us enough to share, we won't know how we can help.

Your apology to Mrs. Malone was heartfelt, and she definitely appreciated it. You love the children and the families, and it really shows in your work. Please work to continue to rebuild that trust with her. We discussed your commitment to keeping family matters private, and I believe that will be the case.

Thank you.
DJ

A Note from DJ

September 29

Dear Beth,

I feel so badly about the challenges at your school. Whenever there's change, there's fear and anxiety. Your staff and families are not upset at you; they are simply concerned about the unknown and need more information.

You told me that the parents expect academic results. My parents here have that same concern. All parents want what is best for their child. My response? Give them the best. Show the parents academic results. Document what the children learn when they collaborate on a project. Identify the counting, sorting, one-to-one correspondence, addition, and other math skills they learn as they play grocery store. Make sure parents understand that the teachers have academic goals for the children and that they organize the environment with those goals in mind. Don't change your plan, Beth. Change your marketing.

Share stories of success. Use successes to show parents not only WHAT the child learned, but HOW the child learned. For example, don't let a teacher send home Bobby's blueprint of an airport without an explanation. Have her explain that while he was drawing it, he was retelling the story of how he and his mom were snowed in at the airport for an entire day. Connect the memory to the drawing and point out that he labeled all the restaurants and the bathrooms. Explain that labeling is graphic representation; a precursor to writing.

Beth, you know as well as I do, that running a school has its ups and downs. Downs happen when we forget that our teachers and parents are as valuable as our children, and we take them for granted or view them as the enemy. Stay connected with your teachers. Meet with parents on a regular basis. You will win this school, I assure you. Go Beth!

PS. I hate having to write this. Cheryl's cancer came back. Looks like it's here with a vengeance. The doctor told her last week that it has spread to her bones. Please keep her in your prayers. She came to Burlington last week, and we had such a great time. She made every child in my school a balloon animal and blew up the balloons on her own; only using a pump once or twice when it was hard to catch her breath. She is simply amazing. The teachers loved her. I'm so glad she came out here.

I'm going to Ohio as often as possible to be with her. Maybe you can join us one weekend for a Girl's Night Out? She'd love to see you again. You are always such fun!

TTYL,
DJ

MONDAY MEMO!

October 3

Rainy days and Mondays always get me down... OK not really. I actually love rainy days! Going outside during rainy days is awesome; especially for children. If there is no lightning and the children have their boots, there's absolutely no reason to stay inside. In fact, I'll put on my galoshes and meet you in the garden yard this afternoon!

At this point, you have had several weeks to extend free play. How is that going for you? I noticed fewer large group activities in most of classrooms last week. When I popped my head in, most of the time the children were busy in their centers. You can tell a difference in the energy (and the noise level!) of a busy class. Please keep this up. Remember to use this time to watch and listen to the children.

A few reminders:

Connie's out this week. I am cooking Monday-Thursday. Hopefully not much on the menu will change, but don't be surprised if by Thursday you see the Domino's guy here!

The garden yard is looking wonderful. I spent time there alone recently. It is such a peaceful place to be. I love it best when the garden is full of children playing and discovering what is in the dirt. Thank you for allowing them the chance to explore! And thank you Kaycee for creating the poster in the front hall announcing, "A little dirt never hurt, unless you're wearing a fancy shirt!" I think the parents got the message!

Have a great week friends!

TO: SUSAN
FROM: DJ
DATE: OCTOBER 3
RE: COOKING

Hi Susan!

Thanks for the offer to cook this week. I have no doubt that you would do a great job; however, the children in your class would miss you! You are definitely a team player, and I am glad you are here with us. Now, go back into your classroom!

DJ

TO: JENNIFER
FROM: DJ
DATE: OCTOBER 3
RE: DOCUMENTATION

Hi Jenn!

I was thinking about our conversation yesterday. I think one of the reasons that Sara's mom is questioning whether or not there is actual "learning" going on in your room is that she doesn't really hear about it. Think about it. Dad drops off Sara at 7:00 before either one of you get there, and when she gets picked up at 3:00, she goes home with Grandma. Mom and Dad really don't get the chance to communicate with you. We both know that wonderful things are happening in your class, yet you don't get many opportunities to share them with the families.

Questions from the parents are an invitation to be reflective. What can you do to strengthen communication? Take your photos for example. You have a way of capturing the children in action. How can you use the pictures with the parents in more meaningful ways? Can you let Sara's family see inside your classroom through your photos?

When you have some time, please jot down some ideas. We can talk again soon.

DJ

Grant: I think the children need more opportunities to tweet in the classroom. I'd like to put a board over the writing center for them to post their tweets. Yesterday a few of them figured out that they could only fit up to 14 characters on a sentence strip. We can teach them the rules and make up user names. What do you think?

DJ I love it! This is both responsive and intentional. Responsive because you are following their lead, and intentional because you are encouraging language and literacy. Go for it!

Grant: Thanks, DJ. I'm concerned because I told this idea to Deirdre and she hated it. I didn't want to go behind her back, but I really think this is the kind of experience you talk about. She's pretty set in her ways about the roles of assistants and lead teachers and thinks I should keep sweeping.

DJ: Thanks for sharing this with me. You have great ideas based upon your observation. I say follow your instincts, and I'll explain that to Deirdre. You are an educated teacher who understands best practices. Don't back down. I'll support you.

Grant: Thanks DJ. Good luck with Deirdre - haha.

Northern Lights Preschool

318 North Harbor Grove
Burlington, VT 05401
555-912-1987
dj@northern-lights-preschool.com

October 6

Dear Mrs. Cagel, Mrs. Wright, and Mrs. Grimes,

Thank you for speaking with me yesterday about your concerns. I learn so much from parents, and your insights brought several things to light. Hopefully this will clear up any misunderstandings.

I agree with you that Mrs. Knox is a wonderful teacher. She adores your children and is always looking for new and interesting materials to bring into the classroom.

I understand that it seems odd for a preschool not to use worksheets or letters of the week to teach, but that doesn't mean we don't teach. On the contrary, teaching is creating experiences based on children's interests and encouraging children to apply their knowledge in ways they find relevant.   This means we do everything possible to individualize your child's education.

Teachers are able to identify how a child learns and modify the curriculum as needed. Worksheets and letters of the week are rigid approaches to teaching that do not consider children's individual styles. Traditional teaching methods use the same approach, year after year, regardless of the children's individual interests or skills. As I shared with you, some children learn, but others just pretend to listen. Many times they act out because they are confused or bored by a "listen-don't-touch" approach or irrelevant content.

I remember once at a dinner party feeling out of place and bored listening to two men discuss their favorite carburetor settings. I couldn't understand, nor was I interested, in anything they said.   I kept saying to myself "Don't let your eyes glaze over. Appear interested. This will be over soon. Oooh, I like that woman's dress. When's dessert?" I can imagine that's how children who are taught things that are irrelevant to them must feel.

By working with children individually, we are better able to understand how they learn and what interests them.   I am a firm believer in this approach and know you will be pleased with the results.

Reading and writing happen in steps. Scribbles and pretend reading are indicators of interest. The fact that your children love to scribble is a good thing. It gives the teachers the insight to incorporate more writing experiences in the classroom's everyday learning. In this case, journaling and tweeting replace worksheets because the children find them interesting. Since they like the activity, they repeat it. When they repeat it, they are strengthening their learning. At NLP we continually seek opportunities like this to extend a topic or deepen the learning for your children.

Please let me know if there is anything else I can do to help clarify what our teachers are doing and how your children are learning. I look forward to seeing all three of you at our Power Hour Literacy Night on November 15.

Best regards,
DJ

A Note from DJ

October 6

Dear Beth,

These last few weeks started off really well. As you know, when introducing change, there are going to be some people who will not buy in at the beginning. Several teachers shared stories of great things going on in their rooms so I assumed that this was the case for all of them. Ha! When some of the moms in Deirdre's class asked for a meeting, I was a bit surprised. (Deirdre is the lead teacher in the Bears.) Remember, this is one of the two classes that has been lauded by the community for its kindergarten readiness program.

Deirdre told parents "We don't do letter of the week or letter pages this year," but didn't tell them what we were doing instead. She also told them that she can't use a curriculum this year and that she was told to teach the children only what they wanted to learn. Well, this explanation didn't sit too well with the moms (can you blame them?) and they are panic stricken that their children will leave the fours room as illiterate hobos. (My paraphrase, but still...)

In this age of accountability our teachers are responsible for identifying specific goals and documenting growth in our children. Letter of the week coloring sheets and projects appear to "prove" that something productive happened in the classroom. However, we both know that it is the experience, not the capstone project, which is most meaningful for children.

Early in my years as a director I couldn't understand why some teachers refused to make the shift from teacher-led learning to child-initiated experiences. I wondered if they thought that by giving the children input into their learning they would lose control over their classroom. I also wondered if perhaps the teachers were embarrassed to admit that the children might want to learn something they knew nothing about. Or maybe they just didn't understand how children learn?

After 25 years of working with teachers, I've determined that those who, after being told about DAP, continue using a teacher-directed approach with young children simply do not understand developmentally appropriate practice. I remember a class I taught last summer for teachers. A teacher of four year olds told the group that she was concerned because a few of her students love to wear costumes all day. She felt that was something that two or three year olds did and she wanted them to act more grown up. This is a prime example of not having a grasp on what is developmentally appropriate. This teacher's misunderstanding led to her stopping the children's play. Teachers need to understand age appropriate skills and behaviors in order to change their approach.

In the past, when two year olds had an altercation, the teachers would say to them, "Use your words and tell her how you feel." I always thought that was funny (as well as misleading), since two year olds don't have a huge repertoire of feelings or words. However, when teachers say, "Tell her that you are mad and ask her to stop," they are giving the children the tools they need to communicate how they feel. In this case, by teaching the children the words (tools), we empower them.

I need to empower my teachers. With the exception of Deirdre, all of them understand the value in child-led learning. They believe me, and they are trying to make a change. What is tripping most of them up is their lack of understanding of children's development. They dote over the children at snack, setting the table for them, and doling out their food: a gesture we do for the toddlers. However, they demand that children sit still or be quiet for long lessons, which is more of a first or second grade skill. Once my teachers understand DAP, the rest of the child/teacher partnerships will work more smoothly.

I overheard Deirdre telling a few moms not to worry about their children falling behind in her class now that I "took away the learning (worksheets and specials)." She told them that she would personally see to it that they were ready for Kindergarten, even if it meant she had to tutor them.

I look at some of these teachers and imagine how happy they will be when they finally relax and enjoy the journey that emergent learning offers them. (I also imagine how happy they would be if I could add a little Xanax to the coffee.)

How's your school?

Let's chat over the weekend. Oh, Cheryl and I are going to NYC in two weeks. We're taking a bus into the city for the day. Shopping, dinner, and a show. Wanna join us? Her attitude is unstoppable, Beth. She is on a clinical trial that makes her weak and tired, but she refuses to slow down. I admire her tenacity. What an amazing woman. You really should come see us in NYC. It'll be a blast.

DJ

TO: DEIRDRE
FROM: DJ
DATE: OCTOBER 7
RE: DISCUSSION WITH PARENTS

Deidre:

It has been brought to my attention that you've shared your concerns about developmentally appropriate practice with the parents in your classroom. This is completely unacceptable and needs to stop immediately.

Deirdre, I understand you are worried that these changes are not in the best interest of your students, and you are unsure that your children will be ready for kindergarten, but you have no right to share this with the parents. Your lack of confidence is causing them unnecessary doubt.

I know that DAP works. NLP is moving in this direction, not just because I believe in it, but because it's been proven that DAP and emergent learning are excellent approaches that successfully teach young children. However, your lack of confidence is going to slow down this process.

You will not grow if you don't give this a try. You are a professional, and I expect you to support this process. I have told you that if you have any concerns come my office and speak with me. Challenge this process; work through your fears, but only in my office.

Thank you.
DJ

October 8

Dear Mom,

Well, the honeymoon is officially over. I'm still struggling to get the staff on board with developmentally appropriate practice. If they don't value the individual child's learning style there, is no way they will create experiences to help them extend their learning.

Parents remember how they were taught in preschools, and teachers feel safe with traditional methods. What I have to do is get parents and teachers to see what I see.

- Children who are treated with respect look at the world with respect.

- Children who are seen as competent and capable see life as a place where they can participate and contribute.

- Children who find joy and wonder in learning become lifelong learners.

I cannot settle for anything less than a school that sees children this same way. I'm not giving up.

Love you Mom!

MONDAY MEMO!

October 10

I want to thank you for your work on building relationships with your children and families. I know it's going slowly, but I can assure you that the time you spend in the first few months of school getting to know the children will be well worth it. If the children trust, you they will take risks. If they take risks, they will learn. Build the trust now. The good stuff will follow.

We've discussed reflecting on your image of the child and the value of respect, but it's time we re-visit those ideas:

I believe that when we treat children with respect, they look at the world with respect. To me, that means respecting their individual needs and interests. It means helping an angry child process his anger without punishment or humiliation. It means ending circle time or any other activity if the children appear uninterested.

I believe that when we treat children as competent and capable, they see the world as a place where they can participate and contribute. I believe that when we show children the joy and wonder of learning, they become lifelong learners. This is what NLP is about.

NLP is fully embracing DAP. It's not what you're used to, but it IS best practice. DAP reaches and teaches every child in your classroom.

For example, if some children become fascinated with puddles, it's up to you to determine how to use the puddles to make connections in other areas. For some of you, this means doing research on water and puddles. For others, it may require you to ask fellow teachers for input.

For those who are stuck in their ways, this may be too much of a change. Some teachers will say, "We cover puddles in April when there is rain. I have some great puddle crafts I will use when we get there." No. Others may redirect the children to see the trees, since it's fall, and it's in the fall that we teach the colors orange and yellow. No! The children don't care about the trees right now! (And most of them already know the colors.) What they want to know is why some of their shoes get really really wet when other shoes stay dry. They want to know how to make a puddle in their tub at home. They want to see if their fish could live in there. That's what interests them now. Let's play on their interests.

One of the reasons teachers may not like this approach is that it requires them to give up a bit of control in planning their day and expects them to collaborate with others.

Something I learned during a seminar in Reggio Emilia, Italy, replays in my head every time I think of developmentally appropriate practice.

"Children can be very stubborn when they are trying to make connections."

To me this means that if we follow the children's interests, we send the message that their questions and ideas are valuable. We want them to look at the world as a place of wonder and adventure; full of puzzles and riddles. We want them to grow up and be adults who will continue to look for answers.

On the flip side, it means that if we move the children away from what they want to learn, we begin an unnecessary struggle. We tell them that they are the receivers of knowledge and the adult is the one who gives. That the adult decides what is interesting.

Sometimes what appears to be bad behavior is a child's stubbornness to continue on his own path of learning. When teachers understand this and plan accordingly, they eliminate 99% of most classroom management issues!

Please continue to observe your children and discover their interests. Then walk along beside them and nurture, grow, and extend those interests. Share your observations with each other and me. Collaboration is crucial for making emergent learning successful. You can't do this in a vacuum.

Go team!

Dear Debra,

I am really glad you took the time to talk to me today. I love your ideas! Creating a print rich environment is not too difficult, although you want to make sure that the labeling is done appropriately. A well-prepared print rich classroom includes opportunities to read familiar words. Here are some tips:

Don't label everything. Too much can be overly stimulating. Don't label every chair. A few will be fine. Photographs of STOP signs and R/R crossing signs in the transportation area are excellent examples of real life print. Menus, recipe boxes, and laminated signs in the dramatic play area also bring authenticity to their learning.

Recycle cereal boxes. Children know their brand of cereal, and will naturally 'read' them, increasing their letter/sound recognition. Use the boxes as a placemat under clay, cut them up and use as puzzles, or as placemats for snack and lunch.

When you label, use a legible font, lower case, unless of course it is grammatically correct. (Joshua Thomas instead of joshua thomas.) Children are taught print before cursive in kindergarten.

Create at least 7 opportunities in the classroom for the children to see their names. When children see their names everywhere they look, it makes them more familiar with letters and sounds. The arrival board is a great idea, as are artist corners for their work, family photographs on the side of a bookcase, a memory game (picture to name matching), on the alphabet tree, around the bathroom mirror, etc.

The idea of a word/picture wall is good; however, I want to offer another option. Instead of covering up the walls with words, what if you created a word chain for each area? Brainstorm some words that might be used by the children while playing in that area. Write them onto little 3x5 cards, and hole punch the corner. Connect them with a key ring, and hang it in the appropriate center. You can add to it as the children learn new words.

I enjoy looking at photos you and Emma have taken. It's so heartwarming to see them active and learning, rather than posed in front of completed projects. It's the process and not the capstone project that's important here. Thank you for continuing to work on that.

DJ

TO: JACQUIE
FROM: DJ
DATE: OCTOBER 12
RE: MISSED BEHAVIORS

Dear Jacquie,

I have an idea about helping teachers understand children's behaviors. I'd like you to think about the misbehaviors in your class as MISSED behaviors, indicating that you missed something the child was trying to tell you. Using this lens, you can look at a behavior as an opportunity to seek what the child needs from you, rather than what the child needs to DO.

Because you were focused on teaching her the "right way to behave", you didn't validate her feelings or suggest alternatives to hitting when frustrated. If Katie can't find the words, ask her to draw what happened, or to show you with the puppets. Or observe her in play so you can see how she connects with the other children.

As with all young children, three year olds have limited experiences to draw from. They need you to offer suggestions. This is true for cognitive as well as social/ emotional situations. In this case, you should have noticed weeks ago that Katie was sad and lonely and helped her fit in before it overwhelmed her coping skills. Had you done so, her behavior may have never escalated to a point where she hit someone.

Once you identify that Katie was lonely, you could offer some suggestions.

"I wonder what Mr. Bear would do if he wanted someone to play with?"

"I have friend named Peyton who is three years old too. Sometimes Peyton gets lonely just like you. She loves to play with the other girls in preschool, but sometimes they are too busy to invite her. Do you know what she did one time? She walked right up to the girls, (I think they were in housekeeping) and asked them if she could play. And you know what happened? They girls said, 'Yes!' They let Peyton join in, and Peyton wasn't lonely anymore. Would you like to try that? I can be right here next to you when you do so you won't be alone."

"My goodness, Katie, I can see that you are really sad about not having someone to play with. I understand what it means to be sad, and I am sorry you feel that way. I wonder if we can come up with something to do that would help you feel better. Do you have any ideas? (no.) Ok, well, why don't we go look in our boredom buster box and see what we can find to do?"

Think about this. Let me know your thoughts. Thanks!
DJ

Jacquie: I love this idea! I was wondering what I needed to be thinking if the children were having challenges, and this brings a whole different light to my self-talk! I love it! Hey, how do I get a boredom buster box? Great idea!

DJ: You and your class together create the boredom buster box. At the start of the year (now is a great time) you all can brainstorm things to do should they need ideas. You present to them, "Sometimes there are too many children working in an area, and someone may need to find another activity. When that happens, what else can they do?" Over time, you and the children can add ideas. Boredom buster boxes are as unique as the classroom itself. Some ideas you may get from the children are:

1. Use the scissors to cut triangles.
2. Look for treasures in the sand table.
3. Hide new treasures in the sand table.
4. Listen to music on the headphones.
5. Play with clay.
6. Set the table for snack.
7. Look out the window and think about things.
8. Measure the shelves and tables with the measuring tape.
9. Draw a story using the idea cube (a die with different animal paws or icons taped on each side. They roll the die and draw a story.)

After you write ideas on index cards, ask them to draw pictures that represent the idea. Eventually children will use the cards without your help. Can't wait to hear how it goes!

Dear Mom,

You are gonna love this! William was brought to my office by a substitute today. Here's our conversation.

Me: What happened, Buddy?

William: I did nothing. Nothing I tell you!

Me: OK, I hear you. Do you know why Mrs. Little brought you in here?

William: Because she is done with me. I am too much!

Me: Honey, if I ask Mrs. Little why she brought you in here, what do you think she might tell me?

William: She might tell you Joshua lied.

Me: OK...

William: But I didn't kick him! I didn't kick Joshua.

Me: OK, what DID you do?

William: I touched him with my foot, little like a butterfly. Like this. (William gives me a little kick)

Me: You know, William, here at this school we call touching someone with your foot like that 'kicking.'

William: Well, then, I did that.

Me: OK. You kicked Joshua.

William: But I was mad. I bet you would be mad at Joshua too because Joshua lied and you're not supposed to lie.

Me: Joshua lied?

William: Joshua told me that he was going to tell Mrs. Little that I was going down the slide head first, but I WASN'T going down head first, I was only TALKING about going down headfirst. But Joshua lied, and the next thing I knew I was here with you.

I asked William what he had done to stop Joshua from being mean and he said "Nothing, I just...kicked him like you said." After we discussed how to handle being angry, I suggested that when he felt the need to kick, he might focus his anger by crossing his legs. He agreed, and thought that was a funny idea. We decided to practice.

Me: OK, William, let's try this. Stand tall.

William: OK.

Me: If you are on the playground and someone says they're going to tell a lie on you, what can you do?

William: I will say "Don't lie. Be a friend."

Me: OK, that's good! What happens if they lie anyway? Now you are mad and want to hit someone with your arms, then what can you do?

William: I want to knock his lights out, that's what I want to do, but I should cross my arms like this. (Crosses his arms) Giggles.

Me: Great! Now, if you feel like you want to kick someone with your feet, what can you do?

William: I can cross them like this. (Crosses his legs) Giggles again. falls over.

Mom, we couldn't stop laughing! It was hilarious!

Gotta run. Love you!

TO: DEIRDRE
FROM: DJ
DATE: OCTOBER 13
RE: HOW CHILDREN LEARN

Dear Deirdre,

Last week you told me that of the 20 children in your class last year, 15 of them could identify every letter of the alphabet. You told me that the worksheets worked to get them to know what each letter stood for.

When I asked you if the children knew the letter sounds, you told me that wasn't your focus, so they didn't learn sounds.

DAP recognizes that four year olds have varied interests in writing and states that children should be exposed to words and letters in the classroom. Teachers support this interest by helping them sound out or spell words when they request help.

It is not developmentally appropriate to teach isolated letters, nor is it appropriate to ignore letter sounds because it is not of interest to you.

By choosing to teach your way, 75% of your children knew rote letters, but had no idea how to use them. If you had used developmentally appropriate activities last year, the majority of the class might have been able to identify the markings and the sounds of the letters in their name.

By doing it your way, they lost out. Your job is to stop teaching as you know it and start creating experiences that foster excitement, joy, and wonder. I'm not going to change my mind about this, Deirdre. Developmentally appropriate practices aren't optional.

Grant's Tweet board idea is a great place to start. Encourage its use as a chance for the children to practice writing. Tweet to them everyday. Model the value of writing and reading and they WILL become interested in doing it themselves. If a child says something funny/interesting/profound, say to the group, "I need to write this down so I won't forget it."

Show them that you love to read and write.

Thanks.
DJ

October 14

Hi Mom!

So Grant's tweeting project is going well. The children write to each other and their teachers almost every day. One little girl checks the tweet board every day to make sure that everyone receives a note, no matter what! How "tweet "is that?

Carol at Learning Kids told me that in order for literacy projects to succeed, her teachers remind the children every day to write in their journals. I don't think they do it right.

The idea behind journaling and tweeting is that the children use this as a form of communication when they are interested. If the teachers have to constantly remind the children to journal, then that tells me the children aren't interested.

In Deirdre and Grant's class, the children initiated the idea of tweeting. They love to write little notes to each other, and they love using the old phones that the parents donated. I think we need to share with the families how the tweet board was created and how the children are learning in the process.

Mom, I am so sad about Cheryl's prognosis. She's having terrible headaches and nothing seems to give her relief. Cancer is so horrible! This is going to be so hard for us all. I plan to go out there as often as possible. I'm sure the school will understand. Nothing is more important than family.

I love you Mom.

MONDAY MEMO!

10/17

(Today's Monday Memo is in shorthand because I am learning to tweet and need to practice.)

Let's C if U no what I want 2 say....

Playground – bikes need to sleep inside

Storage Room – or tornado sight?

Lambs Take Aquarium. (Film at 11)

Staff meeting 10/25   THOUGHTS?

Not sure how to write this one in tweethand, but I need your input nonetheless. The Parent Committee asked if they could plan a Halloween Party for the kids. You've shared with me that several children here don't celebrate Halloween and a loud and crowded school-wide Halloween party can be very overwhelming for the children. What are your thoughts?

Tweet attempt for the above paragraph: Parents' Scary Offer! (Get it?)

Have gr8 week!

@playforaliving

TO: SUSAN AND BARB
FROM: DJ
DATE: OCTOBER 17
RE: ROUTINES AS CURRICULUM

I have been worried about you guys. I know that you are conflicted about what is best for the children and what the parents expect. The answer is simple, although the implementation is a challenge.

It's all about building relationships with your children. Development takes place in the context of trusting relationships. By giving children a sense of security and safety, they feel more comfortable to explore and try new things. When you spend routine times communicating with children, you help them learn to trust and connect with adults.

They need you to show compassion and patience as they self-regulate feeding, toileting, and sleeping habits. They need time. Right now you aren't giving them time. I walk into your classrooms and see you quickly moving through the routines in order to move on to reading, crafts, and other activities. Let's change that.

I'd like to challenge you to spend two weeks focusing on relationships and trust. Slow down the routines. Use this time to talk to the children, to understand their temperaments and their unique personalities. I know you will see how valuable this is for the children and if not I will double your money back!

DJ

(In the meantime, enjoy this little song I wrote for you.)

To be sung to the Simon and Garfunkel's "Feeling Groovy"

Slow down, you move too fast.
You got to make these routines last, just
Take some time to be with me.
(Oops, need a moment…)
Feelin' poopy!

Dadadadah da da da, feelin poopy!

Hello teacher, are you worried?
I'm eatin lunch but feel so hurried.
Ain't cha got no time for me?
Give me those peaches.
Feelin' fruity!
Dadadadah da da da, feelin fruity!

I've got nowhere to go,
No promises to keep.
I'm clean and I'm full and I'm ready to sleep.
and the more time I'm with you my trust it runs deep.
Yep, I love you,
All is groovy!

Deirdre: I read your letter a few times and think I understand what you are saying. I will try to work on experiences that build vocabulary, but what happens if they don't want to write anything down?

DJ: At first they won't want to write anything down. They won't understand the value of writing until you show them how cool it is to write. If you are doing it, they will want to. Remember, the goal is to increase their vocabulary and develop an interest in writing.

Deirdre: How long should I do this, and at what point should I stop and go back to the worksheets?

DJ: You will never go back to worksheets here at NLP. If what you are doing isn't working, you'll need to adjust your approach or try something else.

Deirdre: I'm not sure I have other things to try.

DJ: Don't worry, I have lots of ideas!

A Note from DJ

October 18

Dear Beth,

Do not, under any circumstances, quit that school! You are just going through a hard time. We all have days when everything flows beautifully and then there are the ones like you are having now. Have you reached your goals? Nope, not yet, you just started! Are you still in a position to reach them? Yes, you are. Then this is not the time to leave!

It sounds to me like you are spending a good deal of time fighting fires. Staff shortage is your biggest challenge. You need a few dependable substitutes and pray that your teachers stay healthy. Once you are fully staffed, you will have time to work on other things. Until then, even the tiniest issues seem huge because you must handle them while substituting in a classroom.

Aside from the staffing issue, you said you were having a problem creating meaningful connections with the teachers. That can happen in a school if your day-to-day responsibilities take control. Never forget to work on relationships.

- Commit to being the kind of director that you would respect: smart, fair, honest and classy.
- Make decisions and stick with them.
- Get to know your teachers. Who are they? What motivates them? What are their strengths? What do you notice about them that they don't even see in themselves? Just like a teacher learns about her children, you will need to know their strengths in order to build on them.
- Be present in your conversations. Listen, watch and work to process what they are telling you. No multitasking here. This ALONE will move your staff and families to a place of trust faster than anything else you can do.
- Respond quickly, even if it is to say you are working on it.
- When in doubt, go back to your mission statement. Do your actions/decisions/comments reflect the mission. If not, stop and reflect. Are you going to change your mission or your actions?

Baby steps, my friend. Build relationships, teach, and model. That's your plan. Keep calm and carry on!

Love, DJ

MONDAY MEMO!

October 24

Thank you for coming to me with your questions, concerns, or thoughts about DAP. Your efforts at extending playtime in your room are paying off. Some of you have great stories to share as a result. Please remember that you are on a professional journey. Some steps connect faster than others. The key is to collaborate with other professionals to gain insight on your observations.

I also spoke with the parents re: Halloween party, and they were fine with your suggestions. I told them that you were concerned about having a Halloween party because we have some families that do not celebrate Halloween. I told them that parents are welcome to visit the classroom during free play to read with the children, and that you wanted them to share any hobbies or interests with them. Leah's dad is a publisher. He said he would love to help the children learn about book binding. So, beginning next week, you will begin to see and hear parents asking about how they can become more involved. Looking forward to hearing what comes of all this family engagement!

On a different note, I need to share something very personal. Most of you have met my sister, Cheryl. Others have seen the photos of her on my desk. Cheryl is my very best friend and one of the strongest women I know. In fact, she is my hero.

Four years ago she learned that she had breast cancer. She fought the cancer to remission with all the treatments and surgeries you could imagine. Through it all she kept an attitude of strength and gratitude. Last month we learned that after 3 years the "alien" as she calls it, is back with a vengeance. I will go back and forth to Ohio as often as I can. Thank you for your support during this time. Please keep her in your prayers and I will keep you posted.

Thank you,
DJ

TO: MRS. W, KAYCEE, DEIRDRE, AND GRANT
FROM: DJ
DATE: OCTOBER 25
RE: SUMMARY OF POWER HOUR PLANNING MEETING

This Power Hour will help parent understand how children learn to read and write in a developmentally appropriate, hands on setting. We decided to offer, inside of an hour, a condensed version of the children's day.

Our schedule is:

Begin by telling the parents to find their child's picture and name, and move it to the "I am here!" board. (5 mins)

Post chart paper on each table with the question: what is your favorite memory from preschool? Ask parents to write their answers on the paper. (10 mins)

At 6:15 we enter, look at the board to discover who is missing. After that, we will look at the poster chart paper and read the parents' memories. (10 mins)

We will show how their children have been communicating through tweeting and letter writing. Then we will ask the parents to write a letter to their child that we will put in their mailboxes or tweet wall. (10 mins)

After that we will ask the parents to take a moment to write on their journal paper some thoughts they had about the activity. We then show real samples from the classrooms of what journaling might look like. (15 mins)

We will distribute the articles on how children learn to read and write, then recap our power hour experience by sharing how we translate that into the classroom for their child. (10 mins)

DJ

TO: EMILY
FROM: DJ
DATE: OCTOBER 26
RE: NOTES FOR FAMILIES

Hi Emily,

I have two parent letters here. Please put them on letterhead and add my signature. The first is for the Lambs, and the other for entire school. Please put a copy in everyone's take home bag, and send an email to them as well. I believe this will help the teachers and families.

Dear Parents of our little Lambs:

We are always working to keep you informed of our plans and goals for your children. Susan and Barb have put a great deal of attention to using routines as curriculum. Routines as curriculum refers to the concept that caregiving routines (feeding, diapering and napping) offer an enormous opportunity for the child to learn about trust. Trusting relationships are the foundation for learning and healthy social/emotional growth.

In order for teachers to truly impact your children in positive ways, the teachers at Northern Lights Preschool will spend more classroom time building relationships and less time on take home projects. By spending time with your child individually, teachers are able to determine your child's interests and offer them more appropriate learning experiences. Look for more feedback from the teachers and you will notice an increase in stories about/with your child. Knowledge is power, and we see our parents and children as powerful.

Please feel free to speak with your child's teacher or me if you have any other questions.

Dear Preschool families,

Every so often we will send home a story about something special that happened in our school. While the story may not have happened in your child's room, we believe the practice of sharing our school's stories will help build an overall community here at Northern Lights Preschool. Today I'd like to highlight the Bears' room.

Recently Mr. Grant and Mrs. Knox noticed that the children are very interested in sending "tweets" to each other. They sit on opposite sides of the room, "type" a message onto one of the cell phones, and call out their message to their friend. Some of them even knew the words "hashtag" and "retweet"!

Sensing an opportunity to scaffold learning, the teachers modified the play a little bit, including showing the children how to count (math skills) the characters in their tweets, and how to write a tweet (literacy). They added a vocabulary list to the tweet center and created a "tweet board" with the children's photos and "tweet names." Teachers encouraged students to write/tweet their friends and attach it to the board. The children absolutely love this! Many of them tried their hand at writing and some of them worked in pairs to create messages.

This exciting real-life learning is what we are looking for at NLP. In this case, the children use fine motor, pre-writing, math and communication skills. If you would like to send a tweet to the children, their Twitter name is @bigkidsroom.

Deirdre: It's been over a week and no one cares about writing. I asked them to write whatever they wanted in their journals and they just weren't interested. I even set aside time every day for writing. I honestly don't think this is going to work.

DJ: Stop setting aside time for writing. The experience of journaling should come from them, in their time. Bring it up only when they come to you with something that excites them. Try "Oh, that's a great idea. Would you like to mark it down in your journal so you don't forget what happened?" Do not make writing a center or a requirement or otherwise a big deal and I assure you they will get there.

Jacquie: Brandon came up to me today and told me that when he grows up he wants to be just like Tobias because Tobias never gets in trouble anymore! And you know, I think he's right! Every time Tobias has a challenge now I ask how I can help him and we work through it. I just thought you should know.

DJ: I love that story! I'm glad that you are beginning to understand Tobias and can offer him the support he needs. How did you respond to Brandon?

Jacquie: I told him that my heart had a space in it labeled "Just for Brandon", with a little gate around it so no one else could enter.

TO: JENNIFER AND JACQUIE
FROM: DJ
DATE: OCTOBER 31 (BOO!)
RE: DOCUMENTATION

Dear Jennifer and Jacquie,

Thank you for your support last week during the staff meeting. The teachers needed to hear a few success stories, and your comments helped ease the anxiety regarding all the extra work it takes to document. It's obvious that over the past 6 weeks you have figured out how to integrate documentation and observation into your busy day.

I wanted to touch on your comment, Jacquie, that not all of the documentation should come from the teachers and that you have asked the parents for help, too. I just re-read an article in "Young Children" (March 2008), "The Power of Documentation in the Early Childhood Classroom." The author, Hilary Seitz, says the same thing; "The documentation process is best done in collaboration with other teachers, parents, and in some cases, children, soon after the experience." She also describes the "six stages of documenter experience". I am attaching the article for you, because I'd love to hear your take on what stage you two are at.

You both are doing an excellent job.

Thank you!
DJ

TO: ALL STAFF
FROM: DJ
DATE: OCTOBER 31
RE: CONFERENCES

Hi Everyone,

Ever since our staff meeting, I've been getting lots of great questions regarding the upcoming parent teacher conferences. Hopefully this memo will clarify my expectations.

Conferences are a way for you to share through photos, art, anecdotes, etc. the story of their child's education (child's progress toward lifelong learning). It is not a time to highlight skills taught, shortcomings, or behavior challenges.

In short, the order of the visit is:
1. Show some work, art, photos and share stories.
2. Answer any questions.
3. Hand them the summary and a few of the photos to take home. They do not have to read the summary in front of you.
4. Remind them that at the end of the year they will receive a portfolio with selected works and documentation, plus three self-portraits.

When writing the summaries, use examples that answer the following questions:

How does the child solve problems? Use photos or stories of how she works in the blocks or at the water table, or how he prepares to set the table for lunch. Does he take cues from his peers or dive into a problem on his own? How does the child approach social situations? Is she a leader? If so, have stories or photos to share. Does he wait to enter an activity? Does he have a best friend? Is she the class mentor?

What is the child's unique interest? When he is in dramatic play, does he pretend to be a baker or a policeman? Does he love art, music, and/or language? How do you know? How does the child view himself? For this one, present a child-created self-portrait at each conference. Changes in self-portraits over time are an excellent way to see his self-confidence/self-esteem grow over the year.

I will sit in on your first few meetings to help you get started and can look over some summary reports if you would like feedback. Please let me know how else I can support you in these conferences.

DJ

TO: ALL STAFF
FROM: DJ
DATE: NOVEMBER 8   7:30AM
RE: MISSING PET ALERT!

MISSING PET ALERT! WE HAVE LOST ZIZZY! LAST SEEN YESTERDAY AT 5:00pm. (NOT A GOOD SIGN) I REPEAT. NOT. A. GOOD. SIGN.

Please be on the lookout for our very much loved furry friend. If you have seen a little brown creature, four legs, sweet face, please bring back to Mrs. W.'s room! Thank you!

Tweet@missergrant: Zizzy missing! Tell your kids to check everywhere. Leave no stone unturned as brown one could be him. Reward offered. IDK what just yet. Thanks. (140 characters exactly!)

TO: ALL STAFF
FROM: DJ
DATE: NOVEMBER 8   10:15AM
RE: MISSING PET RECOVERED!

SUSPECT FOUND ROAMING IN THE VICINITY OF THE WATER HEATER. BACK IN CAGE. NEW SIGN PLACED ON CAGE DOOR REMINDING ALL VISITORS TO LOCK IT AS THEY LEAVE. ALL IS RIGHT WITH THE WORLD AGAIN.

Thank you everyone for your efforts!

TO: EMILY
FROM: DJ
DATE: NOVEMBER 10
RE: SOME NOTES

Hi Emily - Getting ready to sleep, but need you to help with some memos. Feel free to make them sound better. Thanks!

To Joey's mom: Thank you for taking the lead to create a goodbye gift for Mrs. W. If there is anything I can do, please let me know. I know that her interests are gardening, square dancing and more recently, roller blading.

To Janitorial staff: I told everyone about your concerns in the back bathroom. Sorry. I can't understand why it always plugs up, either. Also, we are setting up the aquarium in the Lambs' room. Please do not clean near the tank.

To Connie - Pregnant? That is great news! I wish you all the best. Can't you just stay here and let the baby sit on the counter while you cook? Do you really have to leave? (Fix this one, Emily!) Please let me us know your plans.

DJ

TO: ALL STAFF
FROM: DJ
DATE: NOVEMBER 10
RE: POWER HOUR

Hi everyone!

I am looking forward to our event Tuesday night! We have 108 confirmed guests for dinner. While we only officially invited the parents of the fours rooms, some of the threes parents asked to attend. Here is the plan:

Connie and Becca are cooking. The menu includes making pasta with 2 kinds of sauce (marinara and pesto), garlic bread, and salad, milk, water and lemonade. THEY WILL NEED ALL AVAILABLE HELPERS FOR SET UP AND CLEAN UP!!

If you are reading this, you are an available helper!

Susan will make cookies for the children to decorate and some other dessert options, too. (Where do you get the time?) Since it's Italian food, maybe you can make Tiramisusan! (get it?)

Mrs. W, Deirdra, Grant and Kaycee will set up the multipurpose room.

Jennifer will take pictures from beginning to end.

Emily will handle the sign in table.

(Whew!)
DJ

MONDAY MEMO!

November 14

(Before this memo, a word from our sponsor...)

POWER HOUR IS TOMORROW!
LET'S GET READY FOR A NIGHT OF FUN!
POWER HOUR IS TOMORROW!
WE NEED YOUR HELP (YES, EVERYONE!)

I can't thank you all enough for agreeing to be a part of our first ever Power Hour. There's no way we could do this without everyone's help.

(Back to our regularly scheduled memo.)

In Deirdre and Grant's class, Abby and Sean were talking about the day they were born. I thought you might like to "hear" this.

Abby: I was born on a Tuesday from my mom.

Sean: I was born on a Tuesday, too!

Abby: Oh, well, I was born on a Tuesday at the 'Hopsital'.

Sean: I was there, too.

Abby: No, you weren't. I don't remember you there.

(Just listening to the children makes you happy, doesn't it?)

With Thanksgiving around the corner, please remember our plan is for the children to contribute to their own FAMILY meal. That means that your class will prepare enough food for each child to take home on Wednesday. Here is the food list and some suggestions:

Lambs: Mashed Potatoes. The children can scrub the potatoes for a few days, and after they have boiled and cooled off, put them in the big Ziplocs with butter for the mashing. Add salt and pepper to taste.

Monkeys and Lions: Cranberries and Applesauce. This is a variation of my mother's recipe. After boiling the whole cranberries, let them cool. Fill a big bowl with applesauce. Into each quart size Ziploc scoop a 2:1 ratio of cranberries to applesauce, and let the children mix it all together.

Tigers and Bears: Desserts! After the mini pie shells are cooked, the children can add fillings by spooning them into Ziplocs, sealing the bags, and then snipping the corner, so they can pipe the mixture into each tart. You will receive at least 6 tarts per child, so there are plenty of treats.

No, I don't work for Ziploc.

PLEASE SHARE THE CAMERA! I can't wait to see the pictures of the children preparing the food and want to hear about their experiences. If you are too busy to document, please run the tape recorder during the times that the cooking centers are open. This way you can go back and listen to what was going on in that area.

Next week I am going to see Cheryl in Ohio and will return on Monday the 28th. Have a wonderful week and Thanksgiving. We certainly have a great deal to be thankful for.

DJ

TO: ALL STAFF
FROM: DJ
DATE: NOVEMBER 16
RE: PH FOLLOW UP

Hello Everyone!

What a great night! I thoroughly enjoyed our first Power Hour. In just 60 minutes we taught the parents how we approach language and literacy. The activities were perfect and the parents seemed really pleased with the evening!

Connie, dinner was excellent! You and Becca did a beautiful job. Thanks to Susan for those wonderful desserts! Debra, Emma, and Barb: Thank you for entertaining the children! Big hugs to the fours teachers who prepared wonderful activities for the parents and remained calm and collected as they questioned and processed how their children learn language and literacy skills. You guys were great! Thanks, Jennifer, for taking photos. I look forward to seeing them!

It seemed that many parents were comfortable with our philosophy. In fact, it was nice to hear Cassandra Cagle's mom talk about the expectations of Kindergarten and first grade teachers at the school where she teaches. She confirmed that they want children to come to kindergarten with a love of learning and good social skills. She loved the journals and the writing centers, and that both classes plan on implementing them.

We did it! Way to go NLP. Let's keep up this momentum. Thank you, again!

DJ

Hi Mom,

Last night's Power Hour went really well! The teachers seemed comfortable leading the activities. Mrs. W. and Grant were amazing at answering questions. Grant stepped in when a parent asked if the Tweet Board could really teach the children to read and write. Grant's response? "Well, I'm not sure about that, but I know when we did the letter of the week last year, the children only sat down to write when we asked them. Now they go to the Tweet Board all day long, looking for and writing messages." I was so proud of him!

One of the moms asked about projects and why there wasn't as much stuff going home as last year. I swear I almost saw a smirk come across Deirdre's face. But Mrs. W. told the parents, "I notice that on the days when the children are in deep investigation, they are not interested in making something to go home. I moved the project making materials to the art center, so they are still available to those who want to work on them." Then Kaycee piped in with "I wish you all could see how serious the children get when they are investigating. They really like to think. When the bird's nest was found on the ground, they wanted to figure out a way to secure it back on the branch and protect it. We spent several days working on this."

Mom, I had no idea that this bird nest project had happened. Mrs W. isn't quick to share these stories (I think she is just humble), and no one told me. I really need to get these people working on documentation.

Many of the parents were more accepting than I gave them credit for. However, like some of the teachers in the beginning of the year, they understand the research, but just aren't sure they want us to "practice" on their children. I get that. I'm not sure I would stand in line to be a doctor's first heart transplant. I understand the idea of wanting to have what is tried and true. But in this case, Mom, I know this will work! I know this because I have taught this way. I have seen children so absorbed in the life of the millipede that they use everything they have: math, science, writing, cooperation, and problem solving, just to figure out how to save the bug. It's real, it's relevant, the children are excited, and they learn!

One of the moms asked me if her son would still be ready for kindergarten if we didn't teach the letters. That question concerned me. We teach the letters here, but not in the way this mom is expecting. What we need to do is show where the classical learning styles and emergent learning overlap so that the parents can see the connection.

I'm leaving on Thursday for Ohio to spend time with Cheryl. As you know, the headaches have become pretty debilitating and she's having a difficult time with everyday activities. I wish I could be there today, but it's just not feasible now. I will be there soon enough and stay as long as she needs me.

Love you Mom.

Northern Lights Preschool

318 North Harbor Grove
Burlington, VT 05401
555-912-1987
dj@northern-lights-preschool.com

November 20

Dear Mr. and Mrs. Delia,

Emily just shared with me your generous offer to cater our Holiday party! I can't thank you enough! What a special treat for everyone to have delicious food from Delia's Trattoria! We love your food!

Our party is scheduled for Saturday, December 17th at 1:00. In addition to your wonderful lunch we will be having games and activities provided by the Parents Committee. I will have a final count for you by Thursday the 15th. Please let me know what time we need to be available for the delivery.

Again, Grazi! I can't wait!

All the best,

DJ

Deirdre: I know you've been preoccupied with your sister, but I feel like I have to share my disappointment with Grant. He has been trying to take on more and more teaching and planning responsibilities in my class. At first I thought he was just excited about the tweet board, but he's been talking to the parents about their children and bringing in materials for them to play with. I mean, I think it's wonderful that he got excited about tweeting, but he's still just an assistant, right? I mean, shouldn't he stay within those "boundaries?"

DJ: Deirdre, I owe you an apology. I forgot to tell you that I told Grant to trust his instincts and move forward with any experiences he felt might inspire the children. I sensed that he was learning about the children through his observations and wanted to keep his momentum going. Frankly, you are still very concerned that the children aren't learning, and if you take a step back, you will see just how much they have grown in just a few short months.

Deirdre: I need to think about this change, DJ. I was not expecting to move into the role of co-teacher during the year. I have been teaching for many years and until this year have never been told that my methods were less than perfect. It seems to me that since all of the children are still not journaling letters (there is a large amount of scribbling, but not letters) perhaps this is more of a fad rather than an effective approach.

DJ: Let me ask a question, Deirdre. Why did you go into teaching?

Deirdre: I've always wanted to be a teacher. I've wanted to teach ever since I was in Kindergarten. My mother told me that I would read to my stuffed animals every morning.

DJ: You wanted to be a teacher so you could read to the children?

Deirdre: Well, not just read. I guess I wanted to give children a great school experience like I had. I had a great childhood.

DJ: Really? What made it great?

Deirdre: Not one specific thing, really. I stayed at home until I was five and only had "half day" kindergarten at school. I loved my teacher. She let us play. I remember learning to read in her class. We played reading games. Do you remember paint by numbers? We used to do paint by letters. I loved it. I felt so grown up.

DJ: It sounds like you liked Kindergarten because that was where you learned to read. And that's why you became a teacher.

Deirdre: That sounds about right to me.

DJ: I'm wondering why you didn't become a Kindergarten teacher. That seems to be the age you remember and love.

Deirdre: I taught Kindergarten once; a million years ago. I stopped when Sidney was born. When she was old enough to come here, the director asked me if I would become a substitute teacher, and well, the rest is history!

DJ: Do you find there is a difference in being a Kindergarten teacher and a fours teacher?

Deirdre: A little bit. They don't listen as well as the Kindergarteners did. I have to keep the activities shorter to keep their attention, but they are very smart.

DJ: That makes sense to me, Deirdre. You came to this school with the skills of a Kindergarten teacher. And I bet your were a wonderful Kindergarten teacher, because that's what you loved.

What I have learned, Deirdre, is that there is a big difference between four and five year olds, and by focusing on Kindergarten skills in a fours class, you skip over an entire year of developmental goals.

Child-led learning, developmentally appropriate practice, and emergent curriculum are not fads. They are older than I am, and have been successfully implemented all around the world. The schools of Reggio Emilia, in Italy, the Te Wariki approach, in New Zealand, as well as schools in Canada, US, Europe, and Israel all incorporate child-led learning. In each of these communities, I can guarantee that there are teachers, just like you, who are struggling to shift from traditional methods to child-led learning. Like you, they have everything it takes to stretch and move into this approach, but for whatever reason resist.

It's time to give your children the respect they deserve as four year olds, and stop making them act like they are in kindergarten. We are moving forward with DAP in our school. I want you to come along with us.

November 22

Dear Mom,

This teacher, Deirdre, is fighting me tooth and nail. She's been teacher-directed for the past 20 plus years, and while I can understand her trepidation about change, I am done listening to her whine about it.

I could just ask her to come on board and pray that she does, however, that kind of leadership is just not my style. I want to educate, encourage and guide her to do what is best for children. At this point, because she doesn't believe me, she is unable to get to the "educate" part. I have shown her my vision and she has heard about successes with other teachers at this point, so all I have left to do is tell her that coming onboard is the only option. Hopefully she will decide this is the place for her, and if not, well, I'll have to find another teacher.

It sounds so easy to say I'll hire another teacher, but teachers are hard to find. In this case, I would rather run the class myself than have someone drag down the rest of the group.

Oh, the challenges of running a school are both never ending and rewarding. Here's to seeing the rewards soon!

Love you Mom!

MONDAY MEMO!

December 5

Based on feedback from you and the parents, it looks like the parent/teacher conferences went really well. Thank you for trying it this new way! By sharing stories with the parents about HOW their children approach learning, you show them not only that you pay attention to what they know, you are taking the time to see HOW they know what they know. This is very different from years past when you handed them a checklist of skills. Several of the parents told me that this conference left them feeling more connected to their children and NLP. Nice job!

Mrs. Grayson, Randi's mom, was so impressed by a report that included how Randi became more of a leader, with pictures showing her helping the other children put on their coats. She told me that she didn't remember having a conversation about Randi's shyness before the meeting, and was so pleased to know that the teachers were looking out for her. (Nice job Mrs. W. and Kaycee!)

In preparation for spring conferences, please remember that you can share more than just photos with the family. Save children's work and creative projects, write down the anecdotal stories, and maybe try video. Let's give our families a complete picture of their child.

To help you collect and store items for the spring conferences, Emily made portfolio boxes for your rooms. The boxes have hanging folders for each child, and you should be able to store everything you need there. If the children create big items, take a photo of it and place it in the box. All you have to do before conferences is go through the box and select what you want to give parents at the meeting. Remember that conferences paint a picture for the parents. 5 or 6 items, along with anecdotal stories is sufficient to tell their child's story. Leave the rest to go home at the end of the school year.

A quick note about self portraits: In the past you gave the child a mirror and told him to draw what he saw. There is nothing wrong with this activity, but if you want to try something different, here are a few ideas:

- Encourage your children to study a part of the face for a period of time (e.g. eyes). Encourage them to draw their friends' eyes, find eyes in magazines, look at Mom and Dad's eyes, compare them with the eyes of their pets, Zizzy, etc. After a few weeks of this, ask them to draw their self portrait. You will be surprised at the details in the eye area. Continue the study with other parts of the face and you'll get similar results.

- Over the course of a month or two, introduce a different type of media – pastels, watercolors, pencils. Keep those materials readily available so the children can become comfortable with them. When you remind them about their self portraits, make sure those new tools are nearby.

- One last idea. You and your children have been collecting materials outside over the past few months. Why not put them to use and suggest that they make their self portraits using these materials? Or offer sand and glue so they can create a cool sand art portrait? It doesn't matter what they choose to create the portrait. The key here is that you've given them many different ways to express themselves.

If you have some ideas, please share them! Tell me, tell a friend, post it in the potty — whatever works for you.

TO: ALL STAFF
FROM: DJ
DATE: NOVEMBER 29
RE: THANK YOU

Thank you all for your thoughts and prayers for Cheryl. She is a fighter, but it's pretty bad. She never stops working even though she is so tired and challenged by headaches. We still giggle all the time when we are together. I've never met anyone this strong and gracious during a trying time. She loved her visit to the school and still talks about the garden. She told me she wants to come back out soon and have another picnic. I'm glad you all had the chance to meet her.

Have a great day.
DJ

Susan: Do you think I could make cookies for all the children as Holiday presents? I was thinking we could give them cookies and some hot cocoa packets.

DJ: That sounds like a great idea! I'll share it with the others and see if anyone else has something to offer. You amaze me with your passion for cooking. Why did you choose teaching as a profession?

Susan: I've been baking for as long as I can remember. As a toddler my mother used to put me on the counter to help her bake. It's in my blood. I chose child care, frankly, because I've had a hard time finding a great restaurant to work in. My second love is children, so this has been wonderful for me.

DJ: Oh, I see. Teaching is more of a placeholder for you until you can find an opportunity to bake. I don't have a problem with that. It's important to me, though, that you continue to learn about child development and teaching while you are here. I see that you are trying to be more professional and have made strides in what you choose to share with the parents.

I'll see what we can add to the gifts and also keep my eyes open for you. Maybe we can find you a wonderful place to work so you can pursue your passion for baking.

Jacquie: When I first heard you talk about AIR and how you view the child, I thought I'd never be able to do it like you. You made it sound so easy to accept every child regardless of their behavior. But really, it IS easy! I have been asking myself "Why is he or she behaving that way?," instead of taking control and worrying about their manners. I feel like they pick up good habits by watching Jenn and me. To be honest, I kinda wondered how they would learn to be nice and sweet when I wasn't always nice and sweet. Whenever I felt I was losing control, I used to raise my voice. I guess I just didn't know better. Jenn told me she sees a change in the way I act with them. I just think it's easier. Come see us in action!

DJ: Yay! Your note made me so happy! I am glad you are feeling better about your goals for the children. I love that you are having fun. I knew you weren't a mean person. You have such a happy laugh and kind smile. Continue to model the behaviors you want to teach, (make sure they are developmentally appropriate!) and be quick to forgive. And look for my visit sometime this week. I found a great book, <u>The Curious Garden</u>, and I'd love to read it to your class.

MONDAY MEMO!

December 12

Happy Monday Everybody!

I hope that your weekend was wonderful. I spent most of mine outside, enjoying this beautiful weather! Yes, you read me correctly, I was outside! I took your advice to "chill out over the weekend", and I hung outside just reading and relaxing in the school garden. I didn't go into the school at all, but there's something about the garden that centers me. (I told my husband Kevin that I think the garden is what sealed the deal for me moving out here. I don't remember ever seeing a school with such a beautiful, peaceful space.) Of course, now I am running around trying to catch up, but hey...Friday (and winter break) is only 5 days away!

You have some great questions regarding developmentally appropriate practice. Let's take some time to look at your next steps:

This is not an all or nothing curriculum approach. It includes both child-directed and teacher-directed activities. What that means is that you **share** in the learning. If there is something that you absolutely love doing, by all means add it to your day. Your challenge is to figure out how to include it in a way that is developmentally appropriate for all the children in your class.

Look at your current lesson plan. Are you creating lessons in order to teach colors, shapes and concepts? **Stop**. Do you set aside time to teach letters and numbers. **Stop**. Imagine letting the ROOM be the teacher, and you facilitate the action. Let's imagine at new lesson plan. In this one, the goals we work on change from checklist driven skills to skills that lead to independence.

Follow the steps below to help facilitate learning a skill.

1. Introduce (or observe) a sensory experience. Allow enough time for the children to become familiar with it.

2. Add materials to extend the exploration. Make sure the materials keep the activity both challenging and achievable.

3. Take notes and observe for interest, skills or questions.

4. Look at your standards. What are the children's next steps? Keep DAP in mind and consider the specific children you are working with; not the most advanced in the class.

5. Introduce protocol based on the next steps you chose from the standards. Make sure it's challenging and achievable.

6. Create provocations (inspirations) with the goal being independence with those materials or that experience.

For example, imagine that you noticed, during snack, that a few of the children repeatedly build castles out of their apple slices. What can you do with that? This is how it might go down for me:

(Step 1) I noticed that the children used apple slices to make a castle.

(Step 2) Going with the assumption that they liked building part, I would introduce toothpicks and marshmallows during the next snack session.

(Step 3) After observing and asking questions, I would learn that they liked to build with smaller tools in addition to the big blocks.

(Step 4) I would see from the developmental guidelines that they are on target for fine motor skills and double check that the next step is to increase their fine motor skills.

(Step 5) I would bring in twigs and rubber bands to teach them how to build.

(Step 6) Finally, after watching them become comfortable with this new technique, I might show them photos of log cabins, small teepees and other structures made with similar techniques.

Using these steps, you can take any interest and use it to guide their learning in a developmentally appropriate way. I want to caution you not to jump from step 1 to step 6. It wouldn't be a stretch to go from apple snacks to making teepees; however, the steps in between (observing , teaching skills, and creating experiences) are what this teaching approach is all about.

To recap, please keep the following in mind:

- Anyone (teachers, children or parents) is allowed to bring up topics or suggestions for study but they must be okay with occasional rejection of their ideas.

- Introduce concepts through sensory experiences. That puts everyone on the same playing field, and sparks excitement in the topic. (I once had a teacher put frogs in the water table. The children loved 'discovering' the frogs, and were even more excited when one of them jumped out!)

- Share the journey with the families early on. It's okay if the topic goes away after a few hours or a few days. This is what the children were working on, what they were thinking, how they were problem solving, etc.

- Ask open-ended questions that encourage reflection. Take notes all the time about what you are seeing and hearing.

- Offer materials to deepen the learning.

At any time in this process, ask other teachers for feedback and suggestions. You are not teaching in a vacuum. We are on this journey together.

Model the use of journaling.

I'm leaving to go back to Ohio this afternoon. Cheryl's birthday is Thursday and I promised I would celebrate with her. Feel free to email me while I'm there if you would like to discuss these steps to teaching. I want to continue this conversation with you!

December 16

Hi, DJ,

I think I understand now what you mean when you say that we are responsible for teaching the children to be independent. I had a roommate in college who I admired because, at the time, she was the smartest girl I knew. Shannon was an English major who read all the time. She started to read at three years old. However, she lacked many skills. She cried like a baby when she didn't get her way. She would give up on daily chores if the work piled up. I remember her saying that her parents did everything for her. I even remember feeling a little jealous about that. In retrospect, I think that by not making her think on her own and do for herself, she lacked the skills to problem solve or be creative.

I was so impressed with the fact that Shannon was an early reader. Until last week, I wanted to make all of my students early readers, too. I never really considered that teaching meant teaching social and emotional skills, as well. Somehow I lost that connection. I can see now how if Shannon had been taught life skills in addition to reading, she would have been able to handle college life. (She went back home in the middle of our sophomore year.)

I want to give my children the skills they need for life. I understand now what you mean when you talk about lifelong learning. I thought it meant topics like for math and science, but lifelong learning refers to everything they do; including baking a cake or changing a tire. I want to teach the children how to problem solve and seek answers. I understand what you are telling us to do.

I would like to start again with you and learn about developmentally appropriate practice.

Thank you,

Deirdre

TO: ALL STAFF
FROM: EMILY
DATE: DECEMBER 27
RE: DJ'S SISTER

Hi Everyone,

I am sorry to share with you that DJ's sister, Cheryl, passed away yesterday. DJ will be staying in Ohio for a few days and plans on returning to school January 9th.

We are all so very sorry for her loss. Deirdre is organizing the meal making and delivery. DJ has asked that you don't send flowers. You can make donations to the Susan G. Komen Foundation in her name. The website is www.the3day.org/goto/cherylssister

Please let me know what I can do in DJ's absence to support you.

Thank you,
Emily

Dear Mom,

I'm back in Burlington trying to get myself motivated to go back to work. The problem is, I can't do it. My head is pounding, my heart is aching, and I can barely breathe. It all happened so fast and I can't begin to wrap my head around it.

She's gone, Mom.

She was fine when I got out there. We spent a week running errands, shopping, eating at restaurants. Her headaches were horrible, so we just went slow and took breaks. We joked that this was one of the only times in our lives that I was able to keep up with her. We went to her doctor about the headaches and less than a week later she was gone. The cancer took over her brain, Mom. Just like that; my best friend in the entire world was gone.

How can I go back to school with a broken heart and a sadness I can't shake?

God, please give me the strength to go on without her. Please, God, help me make it without Cheryl.

I love you Mom. I miss you, too.

MONDAY MEMO!

Hi Everyone,

Thank you so much for your calls, cards, food, donations and outpouring of love and support. No memo today, just a thank you.

DJ

Northern Lights Preschool

318 North Harbor Grove
Burlington, VT 05401
555-912-1987
dj@northern-lights-preschool.com

January 9

Dear Mr. and Mrs. Hackett,

Thank you so much for your phone call and message. I loved hearing William's voice on my phone when I came back from the funeral. Also, he did something pretty special this morning. When I went into his class, he ran up to me and gave me a huge hug. He put his little hands on my face, looked directly into my eyes and said, "Your sister died."

Me: Yes, William, she did.

William: My fish died.

Me: I'm sorry, William, you must be sad.

William: No I'm not. We bought another one.

Me: That's good to hear.

William: Are you sad, Miss DJ?

Me: Yes, sweetheart, I am sad.

William: (Considered that for a moment.) It's OK if you want to cry. I can sit by you. (He took my hand). Just don't blubber.

Me: Thank you. I will remember that. If I feel like I need to cry, I will come in here and ask you to sit by me.

William: Just call Mr. Grant. I will sit at the lego table in your office while you cry if you want. (He looked at me with deep concern.)

Me: Thank you, William. That is very thoughtful.

William: I know. I love you.

Me: I love you too, William.

William: (Smiling) See ya soon, baboon!

Me: Gotta go, buffalo!

Later on this afternoon he and Joshua brought me some flowers from the garden. They told me the flowers were for the funeral and they wanted me to have them.

William is truly an incredibly thoughtful and sensitive child. Thank you for sharing him with us. He is an angel to me.

All the best,
DJ

TO: JENNIFER
FROM: DJ
DATE: JANUARY 12
RE: DOCUMENTATION

Good morning, Jennifer.

Thank you again for your kind words and support. I am looking over my notes and getting back to work.

When we spoke last month about the photos, you mentioned that you feel like taking pictures of the children in action has almost become second nature. They are no longer posing for you, and you are no longer asking them to. The last photos you took of the children flipping on their coats, pulling up their boots, and wrapping their gifts for their families were really good. I was able to follow the children's eyes and see what they were focused on. Nice job.

You asked me how to best use these photos. The answer depends on your intent because the applications are endless. They can be used to reflect with your children about collaboration or you can use them to document how one child has grown in his self-help skills over the year. You can also take a few photos and document for the parents how their child approaches learning.

Why don't you take a look at the photos of the children flipping on their coats? How can you use those photos to create new experiences that are challenging and achievable?

Let's chat soon. I have some ideas I'd like to share.

DJ

TO: DEIRDRE
FROM: DJ
DATE: JANUARY 12
RE: THANK YOU

Dear Deirdre,

Thank you so much for organizing the team of people who brought meals over to the house. My freezer is full! Kevin and I won't need to cook for at least a month!

Also, thank you for sharing your story about Shannon, and that you now understand the value of developmentally appropriate practice. I look forward to collaborating with you and Grant on whatever lies ahead in the Bears room!

DJ

MONDAY MEMO!

January 16

Hi everyone,

We have a pretty busy week coming up.

Connie is still out for a few more days. She's fine; just needs to stay off her feet for a while. I will cook again this week. No worries... I am beginning to feel pretty comfortable in that kitchen. My goal this week is to only have ONE overcooked item. Anybody want to place bets?

Tomorrow, Captain Jack, the Magic Pirate, will be coming in for a magic show @ 10am. I've never seen him perform, but all of you love him. I'm looking forward to his show!

The staff meeting agenda will be posted tomorrow. As always, please let me know if you want would like to add anything.

Have a great week!

A Note from DJ

January 17

Dear Beth,

First of all, thank you once again for coming to Ohio last month for the funeral. I needed my friend, and it was incredibly thoughtful of you to be there for my family and me.

I miss Cheryl so much. At one point I thought I would just sit down and die, but I'm pushing through. Having 74 children hug and kiss me every day helps make the pain less intense.

On to your question: How do you help a teacher move from one rung on the "ladder of learning" to the next?

The idea of moving a teacher from one place to another can be overwhelming, but we have to do it nonetheless. I tried something with my threes teacher last week, and it looks like it's going to work.

I'd been watching Jennifer, my Lions teacher, evolve from the "Say Cheese" kind of photographer to a candid shot expert. She really likes taking photos and talks about it often to other staff and parents. With the holidays behind us, it seemed like the perfect time to scaffold her into using the assessment tool to start planning for her class. She is the perfect candidate:

- She figured out how to step away from the role of teacher-as-the-center-of-attention to teacher-as-observer.

- She enjoys taking the photos and is motivated to become better at photography.

- She sees, through her photos, what children look like when they are engaged in learning activities and wants to create more opportunities to engage them.

Last week, she and I looked at her most recent photos. Most were of children reaching some milestone...doing the coat "flip", zipping their coat, pulling up their boots, etc. Through our conversation, Jennifer noted that the children are really proud of themselves, and practice getting dressed during center time, even when they aren't going outside. I had her look at the standards to determine the next steps for these children in terms of self-help skills. We spent time thinking about ways to harness this excitement and cross domains. Was there something we could do with math skills? Art?

At the end of the conversation (I guess we chatted for about an hour), Jennifer was so excited. She hadn't realized that reflecting on what is going on in the classroom is at the core of teaching. You could almost see the gears in her head spinning as she thumbed through the developmental milestones looking for a way to assess where the children were based on her photos.

This afternoon Jennifer told me she decided to ask the children, since they are so good at getting their coats on, to create a book to teach others how to get dressed for winter. Jennifer is excited to link their interest in dressing to language and literacy.

We'll see how it goes.

AND LISTEN TO THIS! She told me that she thinks they should have a shorter circle time so they can have more free play because "it's really in the free play where they learn."

Cha-Ching! Another teacher is getting it! I love this.

You know how we always ask the teachers to slow down to teach less material in a deeper and more meaningful way? That applies to directors, too. I believe we need to take each teacher, one at a time, and help him or her move to their next step. Why do we rush them? Seriously, "Whoa Nelly!" should be our mantra.

Don't give up,
DJ

TO: Our Wonderful Tigers and Bears Teachers
FROM: DJ
DATE: January 28
RE: Field Trip to Echo Lake Aquarium

Good morning Everyone!

The trip to the Echo Lake is ready for Wednesday. The bus will be here at 8:45. On it you have 24 children, 7 parent chaperones, 4 teachers and a DJ! I'll take care of the money, Kaycee's in charge of the food and drinks, and Grant has the emergency forms and EpiPen for Toby. The children's t-shirts were delivered Friday and will be given to everyone in the morning. I think we have all the logistics down. Am I missing anything?

If you haven't already done so, please have a pre-trip discussion with the children. Find out what they know and what they want to know about the aquarium. We can add to this while we are on the bus. On the way home we will debrief and see what more they want to learn.

I'm really looking forward to this trip. I've never been to Echo Lake. Can't wait to see all the frogs!

DJ

February 1

Dear Mom,

What a great day! The four year olds went on a field trip to Echo Lake Aquarium. It was our first field trip together. The teachers have a tradition of singing songs and telling stories on the bus. We laughed and sang. I sat next to a little girl on the way there who told me that her dolly had a new baby at home. She's naming the baby Miss DJ. How sweet is that? Then at lunch I helped William open his juice box. He lifted it towards me like he was going to make a toast and said, "Cheers, big ears!"

It was such a nice time watching the children explore and watching the teachers watch the children. I saw Grant write down notes and comment to Deirdre at one of the exhibits. They both had a thoughtful look, smiled, and Grant started writing again. I can see that these teachers are much more comfortable watching and learning from the children than they were when I first got here.

At lunch, some of our children from Mrs. W's class met a few children from another school and they compared t-shirts. Our children asked where they were from. Turns out they were children in the preschool that is part of the homeless shelter. This was new information to our children, who seemed fascinated that these children didn't have a home. I heard Mrs. W. tell them that they could add this to their list of questions when they got back to school. Once she said that, I saw a sense of relief on their faces because Mrs. W. took them seriously and they knew they would get to chat more later. Seeing the children being validated and supported by their teachers made me so happy.

Gotta run. I'm back at school and have to catch up. I just heard that we have an immunization inspection from the health department coming up; which also means that they will be making one of those infamous 5 hour visits soon to check the school and all our paperwork. Ugh!

Love you!

February 6

Hey Mom,

While there were some fun things happening last week, I gotta say we had a pretty stressful January. Of course, I still feel like I've slammed into a brick wall. My energy level is still low and I find myself forcing a smile when I wish I could be curled up in bed crying about Cheryl. I'm so grateful for these teachers and parents. They have really gone above and beyond to be extra cheerful and peppy when I just can't find my pep. And believe me, this month we've needed some extra pep.

My cook is out on bedrest now, and we don't have a replacement. There has been tons of snow, which keeps the children in the building (not the best way to spend a day) and we have had several staff out with winter colds. Somehow we've managed to push through it (we always do!).

Then today something really cool happened that brought a smile back to my face.

Deirdre and Grant TOGETHER came into my office today and were grinning like Cheshire cats!

They told the children about the annual Valentine's card tradition. (They make cards to give to the seniors at Sebastian's.) She asked them what they wanted to do. (You heard right — SHE asked THEM for their opinion!) The children offered up some ideas, including taking the seniors to Ben and Jerry's, then bowling. :) The final, more feasible choice was to visit the seniors at the nursing home.

Grant asked them what they were going to DO for the seniors and after a few more minutes of discussion (clean their rooms for them, bring toys and iPads), they decided they were going to put on a play based on one of their favorite books: <u>Song and Dance Man</u> by Karen Ackerman. It's a really cute book about a grandfather who relives his days in vaudeville and the kids were so excited to put on an "oddville" (as they call it) show for the seniors. They are going to tap dance, tell jokes, perform magic (they were inspired by a magician a few weeks ago) and sing. I LOVE THIS!!

This is so cool.

I love you.

February 8

From: Deirdre

Hi DJ,

I owe you an apology and a thank you.

Last summer, when the parent committee interviewed you, one of the parents contacted a few of us to say that you were completely different than Margaret, the past director. He told us that you were child centered and didn't believe in worksheets or projects. He was really excited about you and your ideas, but he couldn't remember what you said you would put in place of projects or worksheets. This scared me to no end and perhaps made me a little biased before we even met.

I wish I'd never listened to him. I spent part of July and the entire month of August preparing my arguments for why children needed worksheets and teacher-directed projects. Do you remember those books I brought to our first meeting? I was ready to convince you that our ways were best, but you wouldn't listen to me. You never even entertained the idea of worksheets. (I understand why now.)

I'm sorry I gave you such a hard time regarding change. I just wasn't certain this approach was really better than the one I was using. This was unfamiliar, uncomfortable, and, like I said, I didn't give you any benefit of the doubt when you walked in here. After we spoke back a few months ago, I decided to keep an open mind and simply watch the children. Seeing them tweet and send notes to each other, then reading the note Joshua wrote you last month was eye opening. I can see now how one set of experiences leads to another.

Thank you for pushing me to see the value of DAP. It makes so much sense now.

Best,
Deirdre

MONDAY MEMO!

February 13

teeny little monday memo!

Good morning, dear friends,

I am writing this really small so that you would imagine me whispering.

(Shh... whispering...)

We have had a tough month. Snow, illnesses, inspections...I know it's been tough, but all the bad is over now. Let's think about calm. Let's breathe...in..out...in... see, things aren't as bad as they seem, right? We are just going through an itty bitty rough patch. Breathe....

We have a great candidate for Connie's position. (Breathe...imagine someone who knows the lunch schedule and will deliver the food on time.)

Everyone who was sick is healthy now! (Breathe...visualize a school with no more coughing teachers and confused substitutes and our last minute requests for you to stay late.)

The heavy snows are over and we have sun! (Breathe...the children are able to play outside and get some of their energy out - yay!)

Our health inspection is over and we passed with flying colors! (Breathe... no more distracted director worrying about paperwork and immunization records.)

One more little thing: I am canceling next week's staff meeting. We'll have plenty of together time after you come back from your **4 day President's Day weekend break.** :) (Breathe... no staff meeting!)

See, it's all good now. I know you've felt some stress so let's just take some time and appreciate that the worst is over.

To help get you in the mood for your long weekend, we have some gifts for you! Today you'll find a basket of teas and delicious cookies in the kitchen, and "Souper Salad" will deliver lunch tomorrow. Wednesday we will have a bagel breakfast and Thursday afternoon the Parents Committee has a special gift for you. Let's have a great short week, a restful weekend, and come back next week ready for the second half of our school year!

DJ

TO: DEIRDRE AND GRANT
FROM: DJ
DATE: FEBRUARY 14
RE: ODDVILLE SHOW

Hi Guys!

Thank you for one of the best Valentine's Days I've ever had! That was such a great visit to Sebastian's nursing home! The residents seemed to really enjoy the visit and the children were so happy. I loved how you handled Brandon when he ran to the man in the wheelchair. How funny to see him jump in this stranger's lap, calling him Pappa. Who would have known that Brandon's grandfather looked like him?! And funnier is that the man called him son and gave him a big hug right back. I loved it. and I love that you let it happen rather than stopping Brandon in mid jump.

The show was hilarious! And the signs that the children made for Octavia to hold while walking across the "stage" were a great touch. You figured out how to add language and literacy into everyday play! It was obvious that the children made the signs and very helpful that you wrote the actual words under their letters!

I truly enjoyed every bit of the visit. While we don't know what next year's class will want to do, I am secretly hoping we can visit again!

Hi Mom!

You gotta hear this. The coolest thing happened today! Remember in November I told Deirdre to make the decision to either get with the program or leave? I told her I would no longer beg her to do what is right for children. She's the teacher who had that wonderful experience with the children at a nursing home a few weeks ago.

Well, TODAY she came in to tell me she needed to speak with me. She appeared so serious at my door that I just knew she was going to give me her notice. I figured she decided that this approach was just too hard.

Boy was I wrong! She didn't come to me to quit. She came to me to ask me to help her! Yep! We crossed over into the "guide me" stage!! Woohoo! She had a few ideas she wanted to try and asked me to observe her to ensure she was being developmentally appropriate. She also said that she and Grant had been on edge for the last few months because of the Tweet Board, and now that she understands more about DAP she is beginning to feel comfortable again with Grant.

OMG! I was floored!

This is great news. Really really cool. Now that Deirdre is on board, I know she will help bring the parents along.

Love you Mom,
DJ

TO: ALL STAFF
FROM: DJ
DATE: FEBRUARY 25
RE: WHOOHOO!

Great news!

We have a new cook! Her name is Georgia Carson and she's been a professional cook for over 25 years. She worked for the school district until her retirement last year and as you will see, she is a perky woman full of positive energy! We are very lucky to have someone like her with us and I know you will quickly feel the same way.

Enjoy your weekend,
DJ

A Note from DJ

March 6

Dear Beth,

Wow, what a long letter! It sounds like you and your staff had some winter blues, too. Thank goodness spring is around the corner. Life always seems better when the sun comes up. In the meantime, let's break down some of those challenges:

1. You were making some changes for next year, decided to let someone go, told a teacher, asked her not to tell the others, but she did. Live and learn my friend. You are the leader of that school and you are not to share secrets with anyone on that staff unless you are okay with the rest of the staff hearing about it. Call me, or talk to a local director. We can keep secrets.

2. You have a teacher who was consistently late all year long, but only now you seem really upset about it. The difference is that this time it affected your ratios and licensing came in before the teacher got there; causing you to get a violation. My suggestion for this one is the saying "See it, Say it, Stop it." This is something I learned my first year as director and never forgot. When a teacher behaves unacceptably, say something right away and let her know that you will not allow it. The opposite of this is "See it, Slide it, Sanction it." You choose.

3. As for the parents who want input into your curriculum: to me this means your parents are invested in the school (yay!) and you need to work on creating a shared vision. Everyone needs to be on the same page about developmentally appropriate practice and child-led learning. Once they are, no one will ask to have input into your curriculum because they will understand and agree with your approach.

Look at the documentation and other communication that is being shared with the families. It seems to me that when teachers stop their usual activities (worksheets and letters of the week) but don't replace them with alternative proof of learning, families have nothing to hold onto. Make sure there are photos going home showing what is happening in the classroom and that the notes and flyers they send talk about how the children learn.

Notice that each challenge you shared with me had an answer. Look inside when you seek answers. Ask yourself: "Where was the communication breakdown?" "What can I do differently?" "What systems need to be put in place?" Looking at the challenge from a point of responsibility will help you find the answers faster.

All leaders make mistakes, Beth. It's how we learn. Don't be so hard on yourself. You have what it takes to make this work. Just keep pushing.

Love,
DJ

TO: GRANT, BARB, GEORGIA
FROM: DJ
DATE" MARCH 12
RE: TACO NIGHT SING ALONG

Hola! Hi Grant! Hi Barb! Hi Georgia!
(Now to be called the Three Amigos!)

Thank you for taking on Taco Night. I think this is going to be a great event!

Here is what we have planned:

We will send home invitations next week to all our families and potential NLP families next week.

All the classes will pick their favorite songs and the four year olds will write them down on a tweet board (with some help from their teachers). After dinner, Grant will pull the tweets and place them on the easel and Barb and her guitar will lead the sing-a-long.

As for dinner, Monkey and Lions will hand-tear lettuce, and the Tigers and Bears will cut up tomatoes and shred cheese. We can probably expect close to 200 people, so Miss Georgia is going to prep the rest of the food.

Dinner will be served family style in baskets on the tables. I'll ask Susan what she thinks will be a good dessert. Any suggestions?

Hasta la vista!
DJ

A Note from DJ

March 17,

Dear Beth,

I'm glad things are falling back into place. You did a great job with that teacher. "See it, Say it. Stop it!" Yay you! It's gotta feel good knowing you took control over her tardiness. Just remember to follow through. If she's late again, write her up just like you told her you would.

Every year around this time directors begin to ask the same question: How do you move a teacher who doesn't want to be moved? This is usually because they have spent the fall creating relationships and sharing new information with the teachers. Then they spend the winter months working along side them, modeling behaviors they hope will soon catch on. Many teachers begin to show interest in making change by now. But there is always at least one who still seems reticent.

How do you get her past "I already do that" to "that's something I'd like to try"?

My answer to you is in the form of a question. Why do you want to move a teacher who doesn't want to move? Why are you trying to get her to play nicely in your sandbox if she really doesn't want to be there?

As directors, we have to determine which teachers we'll work with and which ones are not proper fits for our programs. It's a delicate task and sometimes we are wrong. Just like some children respond better to certain teachers, some teachers respond better to certain kinds of leaders. My best advice to you: if your gut tells you this teacher is worth fighting for, don't give up until you've exhausted your bag of tricks. At the same time, if you decide that a teacher is not a good fit then start the search for her replacement.

I know what your next question is: What's in that bag of tricks, DJ? Here are a few of my favorite ways to help move a teacher along.

Promote: Teachers need to know your vision. Take them on field trips to model schools, show videos of best practices, bring in slide shows and speakers from schools that share your vision.

Educate: Introduce them to the research behind your vision. Offer them articles, start a book club, meet them one on one and encourage them to join a networking group of like-minded teachers.

Model: Your vision is based on your values and expectations of how young children learn and communicate. Model those expectations and values in your school. When you enter a classroom, be respectful. When you plan staff meetings, make sure the info is relevant to every teacher. Be reflective when they come to you for support.

Differentiate: Remember that every teacher is not a mini you. You, my friend, are an informal person with a great promoter personality. For you, my enthusiastic responses are enough to get you going most of the time, but other teachers may think differently from you. They may still make wonderful teachers, but watching you jump up and down is not going to move them. Share your vision, help them see how it connects to them, and then answer their questions. Respect that they may move slower than you and accept their methodical nature. If you are seeing changes, even a little at a time, you know they are on the path.

Lead: Tell your teachers what behaviors are not acceptable at any time. When you see it, say something. If you let it slide, you are sanctioning it. Don't be scared to stand up for what you believe in. You are in that school because you know what is the best environment for young children. Make sure your school reflects that.

After you've put in sufficient time and effort and have supporting documentation, you can determine whether or not to keep that teacher. Until then, keep plugging along. Sometimes all it takes is a little switch to click on for them to come on board. It happened that way for Deidre and I'm very glad it did.

Thinking about you and your staff.

Love,
DJ

Northern Lights Preschool

318 North Harbor Grove
Burlington, VT 05401
555-912-1987
dj@northern-lights-preschool.com

March 18

Dear Parents,

Thank you for your support as we navigated through some changes in our school this year. Looking forward, fall registration starts next week! Soon you will receive your registration packets.

Professional development is a key factor in quality early childhood education. Our teachers are remarkable people who want to continue learning from and networking with other professionals. In the past, they have been given three days of professional development in the beginning of the school year. We have elected to add three additional days to next year's calendar for training opportunities. NLP will close on those days.

Because of this change, next year's tuition rates will stay the same. The revised calendar will be in your packet. Thank you for understanding.

Please let me know if you have any questions.

All the best,

DJ
Director, Northern Lights Preschool

Hi Mom!

Something may be going on in Deirdre and Grant's room. One of the four year olds brought in a picture of the Northern Lights. Grant said the children were very interested in it and he wants to know if this could turn into something good. He said Deirdre was talking about researching a craft project using the lights, but he remembered me saying not to jump quickly to a capstone project and wanted to know what to do instead.

I. Love. Grant!

I told them to just relax and watch the children for a while. I remember a teacher once who wanted a dollhouse in her room so badly ("They LOVE the dolls, DJ, and need a dollhouse") that she kept pushing the kids to create little houses out of cardboard, sticks, and cloth. While that was fun, it was NOT because the children wanted a dollhouse. They just loved the different ways to make houses. I saw that. I wish the teacher had seen that.

As for the Northern Lights photo, Grant and Deirdre need to watch and listen to the children first to see if any interests come to the top.

I'll keep you posted. I Always do! Love you Mom!

TO: JENNIFER
FROM: DJ
SATE: MARCH 28
RE: JACQUIE

Dear Jennifer,

Thank you again for coming to me regarding Jacquie. I believe you when you say that you see a change in her approach with the children and feel confident that she is beginning to use Absolute Intentional Regard.

You have been one of Jacquie's biggest supporters. When you came to me in the fall to share your concerns, I knew that you saw something wonderful in her. She's lucky to have you as a colleague and a mentor.

Let's continue to work together and make sure that class has nothing but the best environment with nurturing teachers!

Again, thanks,
DJ

TO: DEIRDRE AND GRANT
FROM: DJ
DATE: APRIL 1
RE: NORTHERN LIGHTS PICTURE

Hi Guys!

I heard about the picture that Jeremy found at his grandpa's house. That's so cool! I think you are on the right track. This could turn into something very exciting.

Just a few reminders from Margie Carter and Deb Curtis' book <u>Reflecting Children's Lives</u> as you get started:

- Seek the child's perspective. We want to meet them where they are so we can help them move forward. Ask questions, probe, and document what you hear.

- Remember that it may take a little time to determine what interests the children. Keep notes that you share with each other as you go along.

- Look for something that speaks to your heart, too. Enjoy the process.

- Take lots of pictures. When you revisit them, you will be better able to see what the child was seeing.

- Involve your families. They may be more supportive than you can imagine. (OK, that one was mine, but keep it on your list!)

Please let me know how we can help you. Good luck!

DJ

Hey Emily,

I told Deirdre and Grant that we would support "Operation Northern Lights" anyway we could. The children are very interested in this topic and are trying to understand how things can simply fall from the sky without hurting people on the ground. Please warn the cleaning crew that we will encourage the children to do some off-the-wall things; like throw confetti and small paper. This may go on for a little while…

Also, can you please print the pictures from their camera every afternoon? I will begin documentation to share with the families.

I am so glad we got those cameras from the parent committee!

Thanks, Emily!
DJ

TO: MRS. W. AND KAYCEE
FROM: DJ
DATE: APRIL 5
RE: FUNDRAISER IDEA?

Dear Mrs. W. and Kaycee,

I love your idea about a fundraiser for the homeless shelter's preschool. The fact that the children came up with the idea to help the shelter makes this all the more exciting. Have they decided what you are going to sell?

I remember years ago making jewelry with puzzle pieces. The children painted them a solid color and glued them together to create pins. Once completed, they glued on pin backs and then splatter painted them. The process took a few weeks, but the "jewelry" was beautiful and sold really well.

Please let me know if you need any support on this or any other project you and the children choose.

Thanks!
DJ

MONDAY MEMO!

April 9

Good morning!

This place is rockin'! In case you haven't noticed:

The Tigers are raising money for the children's preschool at the homeless shelter. Please bring in any puzzles you have lying around at home. They don't need to have all their pieces.

The streamers in the hallway are part of Deirdre and Grant's project **Operation Northern Lights**. Feel free to take a field trip to the hall with your children. Turn off the hallway lights and lie on your backs for a minute to see the moving streamers. It's really cool. If your class wants to get involved with this project, they are welcome to collaborate. Just chat with D or G for details.

Did you notice all the paint on the lower half of the playground doors? That is the talented artistry of the Lambs! The teachers decided to give the children a new space in which to be creative. In small groups they went into the hallway, dressed only in their bottoms, to either finger-paint or sponge paint the door. It cracks me up every time I go by there, because the colors end about 2 feet off the ground!

In case you were wondering, no, I'm not concerned about paint all over the back doors. This is a preschool. Where else would two year olds be given the chance to paint on a door?!

Have a great week!

MONDAY MEMO!

April 16

Hello Everyone!

It's been well over a month since we had a reason to bring in lunch for everyone so I have decided to create a reason.

Since this place has amazing things happening everywhere you look, and because the Circus is in town, we will celebrate 3 Ring Thursday! Yummy food that will give you energy to continue your great work!

Breakfast will be oatmeal with lots of great toppings (including Mrs. W.'s favorite caramelized walnuts).

Lunch will be a salad with mesquite grilled chicken and garlic sticks. (Thank you, Georgia!)

For an afternoon snack, the entire school will share a sundae bar in the gross motor room. We have lots of great toppings for everyone! Come on over after nap! We'll have a picnic on the floor.

Yum!

See you then!

TO: ALL 4'S TEACHERS
FROM: DJ
DATE: APRIL 21
RE: GRADUATION

Hello Friends,

It's time to talk about graduation. This year we have 3 children who won't graduate because they did not make the kindergarten age cut off. This new information caused me to look at graduation with a more critical eye.

I'd like to re-visit the manner in which our four year olds say goodbye to NLP. In the past, you had a formal graduation ceremony with caps and gowns and 30 minutes of music and presentations. A few of you have shared that graduation is too stressful because the children have to memorize their songs and practice lining up and sitting down.

We've been together for close to 9 months so I am sure you can guess where I'm going with this memo. I want you to think about these questions.

- What is the intent of graduation?
- What messages do we want graduation to send to the children and their families?
- What parts of the ceremony, as it currently stands, are developmentally appropriate?
- What parts of the ceremony, as it currently stands, are relevant to the children?
- What parts of the ceremony do the children own? In other words, what decisions did/will they make regarding the ceremony?
- If you were able to recreate this tradition, what would you want to keep, what would you toss, and what would you add?

I look forward to hearing your comments and suggestions!

Thanks!
DJ

Northern Lights Preschool

318 North Harbor Grove
Burlington, VT 05401
555-912-1987
dj@northern-lights-preschool.com

April 21

Dear Parents of our Fours Classes,

I hope this letter finds you well. It is hard to believe that the school year is almost over! Our last day of school is June 1. This means that it's time to talk about graduation!

As many of you know, past graduations were evening activities and the children wore caps and gowns that you bought. (They cost about $20, but made great dress up clothes!) At the event, the children sang some songs and one by one received their diplomas. It ended with, of course, cookies and milk!

This year, I would like your input regarding the **Northern Lights Preschool** annual event. The teachers and I are re-evaluating, as well. We are wondering:

What does a preschool graduation mean to you and your family?
What would you like to see happen at a graduation ceremony?

Thanks for your input. Feel free to email, call, text or tweet your responses: dj@northern-lights-preschool.com, 555-912-1987, @playforaliving

Have a wonderful week!

DJ

MONDAY MEMO!

April 23

Spring conferences are coming up! I've chatted with most of you about your portfolios; however, if you need anything at all please let Emily or me know. Remember, the goal is to paint a picture of HOW the child learns, not WHAT he learned.

Also on the radar this week:

Emily distributed your letters of intent for the fall. If you are interested in coming back (and I hope you are), please return them as quickly as possible. Remember, you are able to request different age groups, different co-teachers, or different classrooms; just not a different director. I am going nowhere. I love this place! While I may not be able to accommodate everyone's request, I will do my best to work something out with you.

And now a word from our sponsor: Mrs. W. and Kaycee are pleased to announce the beginning of their classroom's fundraiser. Zizzy's class has designed and created beautiful picture frames and jewelry from repurposed puzzle pieces and popsicle sticks. These lovely gifts are sure to be a hit with all the fancy and hip people in your life.

Everything is $5. I know you have $5! You got paid last week! Think about all the people in your life who would love a thoughtful gift. All proceeds will be donated to the homeless shelter's preschool. Please share the love and tell your friends. Free shipping if they pick it up here! (OK, so no free shipping!)

Have a great week!

TO: DEIRDRE AND GRANT
FROM: DJ
DATE: APRIL 23
RE: BENCH?

Hi there,

Rumor has it that your classes are decorating a bench for their graduation gift! (OK, maybe not a rumor.) One of your children, who shall remain nameless (although his name rhymes with Billiam Lackitt), ran up to me this morning and whispered, "We have a secret bench and can't tell no one but missergrant and deedra!"

I offered him a few cookies and got the rest of the story. (Pretty easy if you ask me!) Anyway, thank you so much for such a thoughtful gift to the school!

I know this will cost a pretty penny. Can NLP pay for the bench or the photo developing? Please let us defray some of those costs.

I promise not to watch your class work on it.

I promise not to look in the sand table for all the pictures (Wow, cookies can get you so much information).

And I promise not to tell another soul.

All the best,
DJ

TO: 4'S TEACHERS
FROM: DJ
DATE: APRIL 24
RE: GRADUATION

Hello Everyone!

Thank you so much for your fast input on graduation. Based upon your answers and the parents' responses, it looks like we are going to have a ceremony, certificates, and a celebration, but not necessarily in a formal setting. Here are the final three options:

1. Children have a "growing up" ceremony, receive certificates, and eat cookies.
2. Parent/Child sing along with certificates and cookies.
3. Daytime lunch and ceremony with certificates.

Please let me know your thoughts before tomorrow afternoon. It's time to make a decision!

Thanks!
DJ

April 24

Dear Mom,

Oh.My.Gosh. You would not believe the responses I have been getting from the parents regarding preschool graduation! Almost every parent weighed in. You would have thought this was a primary election!

Hands down, the parents want something to signify that their child is leaving NLP. As one mother put it, "This is really for me, too. I've been here for 3 years and kinda feel like I am the one graduating!" Almost everyone wants an event that is cost-free and less "staged."

A few parents didn't really care what we did, but were quick to thank me for asking their input. Apparently that was not done in the past and they love the level with which we have involved them this year.

Most teachers wanted something light and fun. Only one thought that the practice and rehearsals were worth the trouble --"it looks so great and the parents love it." She also acknowledged that she and the students would have more fun without all the stress of rehearsing.

What everyone wants is a ceremony that is meaningful to the children and recognizes that their families are graduating, too.

The school normally closes at noon on the last day for graduation. We decided to have a brief "growing up" ceremony followed by a school-wide carnival. How can you lose? We will ask the four year olds to think about what they want to be when they grow up and to create something that represents what they are thinking. Their spotlight moment will happen when they share what they want to be. Then they will each pose for a photo and move on. There will be certificates to take home and a carnival in which to party!

The teachers are so excited! Since they realize that the parents are fine not having a formal ceremony, all of the pressure to perform is lifted. They may get involved in the costume creating or the stories the children tell, but I know that the children will own a large part of this event. That's a NEW CONCEPT for this little school.

I couldn't be happier.

Love you Mom!

A Note from DJ

May 2

Dear Beth,

Wow, what a month! Deirdre's class had a true emergent learning experience! From the initial interest right down to the documentation, every step was beautifully done! You are going to love this.

Jeremy Booker came to class with some photos he found at his Grandpa's house. It turns out they were photos of the Northern Lights. The children got very excited about the Northern Lights (since that's the name of our school) and started talking all at once. No one had seen the Northern Lights but Leah told the class that her daddy saw the lights before she was in her mommy's tummy. Deirdre and Grant decided that this could be an interesting course of study. They worked together! Can you believe it? Grant listened and Deirdre went to the reference library for some books. She shared the book Northern Lights A to Z by Mindy Dwyer. Afterwards, she asked the children what they knew about Northern Lights. Here's some of what they told her:

- "It's not really lights, but stars."
- "God colors them in before they fall."
- "They took the name from our school's name." (loved that one!)
- "The clouds hold them until its time."
- "They are really rain."
- "Sometimes its purple or green or blue, but never black. Black is for nighttime."

Deirdre and Grant observed the children for the rest of the day. Several children started to paint and draw their interpretation of the lights. Jeremy compared the photographs from the book to the photo he'd brought.

It was clear to the teachers that the students were interested. Deirdre emailed her colleagues and the parents, shared what happened, and asked for their ideas and help. (Yep, she asked the parents for ideas. I am so proud of her!)

Then many cool things started to happen:

The next day Deirdre brought flashlights. She showed them to the children and asked how they wanted to use them. After they played with the on/off button for what seemed like forever, the children started asking questions. They wanted to know if they could make the beam of light from the flashlight colored. They asked if the colored lights were only there at night. They also wanted to know if people on airplanes saw the lights.

Devon's dad brought a telescope that added to the interest in looking at the sky. Some children wanted to make their own telescopes, so that became the next project. Deirdre encouraged them to draw plans before building them, so the children designed telescopes. (What traditional preschool designs telescopes?) Their drawings were incredibly detailed.

Deirdre and Grant put aside their lesson plans and became facilitators. For example, in the block center, some of the boys were building a tower. They were focused on making it as tall as possible. At one point, when they had pulled a chair to stand on, Grant asked them if they needed his help. They announced that they wanted to make their "ladder" bigger and take it outside so they could touch the lights when they come back around. Building stopped while they discussed how far the sun and the sky were from the school. When the children learned that there were not enough blocks in the room to make a ladder reach the sky, they decided to go in the hall with their blocks and make their ladder as LONG as they could.

Jeremy's mom came to class and explained, as simply as possible, how the lights are not really lights but particles from the sun that get trapped in the earth's magnetic field when they fall to earth. The children were surprised that particles meant dust and began speculating how the sun gets dust on it. "Is rain when the sun takes a tubby?" Great question!

Leah's dad made quite an impression on the children. He explained that he saw the lights when he was living in Montana (which took the children on a little side study of the U.S. map). He also shared that he was walking down the street one night and was surprised by the lights in the sky. He said it looked like God was shaking a blanket of color over the sky. Someone asked him if he took a picture and he told them no, but that he would remember it in his heart forever. Deirdre said the children simply stared at him and nodded their heads in understanding. After he left, some of the boys started showing each other how to shake a blanket to make the colors wave. Jason began making up stories of what he would do if he was walking all alone down the street. (Gotta love how some kids see different perspectives of a story!)

The children wanted to make blankets of color. The weaving tool, which hardly gets any use, became a staple in the classroom, and we actually had to buy more loops!

Grant showed a few children that if they punched holes in a black sheet of construction paper and lifted it to the light, it looked a little like the night sky. This new idea was a winner with several children who practiced hole punching and scissor cutting. One child cut out a large portion of the black paper and decided to lay it on top of green paper to make the colored sky. All the children were excited about this and joined in.

Leah's mom brought in crepe paper, and the children told Grant how to arrange it on the ceiling to make the colors "shake". One of the little girls asked if birds could get hurt when this happened.

Teachers posted photos every day. They ran a slideshow on their computer so the children could revisit them whenever they wanted. They put posters with streamers and photos in the hallway so the rest of the school could share in their learning.

Beth, this process of discovery has gone on for almost 4 weeks! The classroom and the hallways look like an astronomy museum. Now other teachers are interested in doing this with their classes. There's a different, more powerful excitement around here! I think some people just needed to see it in order to believe it.

I am thrilled to bits. I can't wait to see what happens next!

DJ

"I have observed over and over again that young children, who are intellectually engaged in worthwhile investigations, begin to ask for help in using academic skills - for example, writing and counting - in the service of their intellectual goals." ~ Lillian Katz

Dear Deirdre and Grant,

I've enjoyed watching your class this past month. "Operation Northern Lights" was a success because you embraced developmentally appropriate practice. Quite frankly, the project could have fallen flat many times had it not been for your commitment to the process.

For example, when Jeremy shared the photo from his grandpa's house, you could have easily thanked him and dismissed it; stopping him in his tracks. But you didn't.

You both saw and respected that the other children were interested and you followed their lead.

You understood that this was something worth investigating in depth and you decided that involving others was more important than keeping total control of your class.

Emailing the staff and parents about the children's new interest was a brave move. It allowed those of us who are outside of the classroom and the parents to become part of the experience. I'm proud of you.

After Leah's dad shared his story, when the boys were shaking the blankets, you could have easily stopped them, using "safety and inside rules" as your excuse, but you didn't. You kept an eye out for potential dangers, but allowed them to try. I believe this led to the very popular weaving experience.

You understood that children who are allowed to seek answers will continue to ask questions, and you made it possible.

Grant's demonstration of hole punching reinforced the idea that even the grown-ups get excited about learning. You could have easily directed a project that utilized hole punching, but you didn't. You taught them a skill, and allowed their excitement to drive their learning.

You saw an opportunity to scaffold their learning and allowed them to make discoveries on their own.

When Leah's mom brought in the streamers, you followed the children's direction to hang the streamers up on the walls. You easily could have said "enough is enough already," but you didn't. You joined their excitement, understood their intent, and helped them see their vision through.

What you did, my friends, was honor their children and helped them facilitate their own learning. At any point you could have stopped. You could have gone back to your lesson plans, but you didn't. The result was a month of magic that taught math, science, social studies, geography, astronomy, literacy, and art.

And for that, on behalf of the staff, children and their families, I thank you.

Regards,
DJ

TO: ALL STAFF
FROM: DJ
DATE: MAY 6
RE: SEPARATION ANXIETY COMMITTEE

Hello Friends!

In preparation for next year's incoming families, I have decided to take your advice and create a group that helps parents and children at drop off.

As you are aware, most of the challenges you face at drop off are instigated by parents or children who don't want to separate. You have shared that the parents stay in the room with their child causing the room to feel a bit claustrophobic, as well as, adding to the overall noise of the morning routine. Many of you have commented that the parents wait until an inopportune time to leave, which sparks tears from their child who may have been fine with a typical drop off routine.

Asking parents to leave can be a touchy topic. As employees of the school, sometimes we represent the reason parents are sad. I thought perhaps a group of parents who have all "been there, done that, survived" might make it easier.

The Separation Anxiety Committee will be made up of any parents who are interested, but specifically parents who had a challenge in the past separating from their children at school. Volunteers from this committee will meet with parents who may need a little support, drink a little tea or coffee, and help them feel comfortable leaving their child.

Please help me identify committee members. We will talk to them now to ensure they are ready for the fall.

As for the children who have separation anxiety, I will leave that up to you; the experts. You know how to calm your children and engage them in meaningful activities. I'll take care of the parents!

Thanks!
DJ

MONDAY MEMO!

May 7

Good morning, Burlington! (I saw Hairspray on TV last night and couldn't wait to sing that to you today!)

There are only 4 more weeks of school! Only 4 weeks for unlimited hugs. Only 4 weeks of wide-eyed wonder and amazement. Only 4 more Monday Memos! We are soo close! I know it's getting a little crazy in your classrooms. Maybe it's boredom or the full moon, or springtime hay fever causing it, but consider this:

For teachers, with only a few weeks left, some of you may decide not to work on big projects because well, school's almost out. Some may decide not to bother with new and fun materials right now because any new things you come up with can be added to the fall. Or maybe you have been inconsistent about the children's behaviors, resulting in slightly fewer boundaries because hey, why not? You may be thinking, "School's almost over, let's just write off the year."

The children will be confused by the changes. They don't understand what's going on and may think that now they can behave a little crazier. Then they are hurt when they get in trouble because they were "too wild." Or maybe they are bored because you haven't given any new challenges for them to think about, so they will cry or fight just to get your attention.

This scenario is being played out in preschools everywhere. My job is to remind you to stay on track just a little bit longer and continue to give your children the same thought provoking and engaging experiences they've had all year long. I am right around the corner if you need ideas or want to collaborate.

Some of the children in the Tigers and Bears have expressed an interest in naming the Garden yard. Mrs. W. has offered to take charge of this activity. If you have any suggestions for names or how to vote, please share your ideas with her.

Mother's Day is this weekend. If you are looking for that perfect gift, I hear puzzle piece pins and picture frames are on the list of every mom in Burlington!! Lucky for you, Mrs. W. just told me that the children have plenty of inventory. So far they raised $340 for the preschool at the homeless shelter! Keep it up!

MONDAY MEMO!

May 15

Hello Everyone!

It's time for voting. Thanks to the Tigers, who used their tried and true market research methods (clipboards and in-the-hallway interviews), we have narrowed down the names of the garden yard! You have three choices. They are:

1. The Garden Yard (we have some minimalist thinking going on at this school)
2. The Garden of Eating
3. The Curious Garden

Voting closes at 3:30 on Wednesday. Please bring your children into the multi purpose room sometime over the next few days to place their votes. The Tigers created little stickers with the names on them. Your children need only to pick a name, stick it onto one of the cut out leaves (thanks to the Tigers and Bears for cutting out all those leaves), and place their vote into the picnic basket on the back table. We will announce the garden's new name at our board meeting on May 23rd.

Northern Lights Preschool

318 North Harbor Grove
Burlington, VT 05401
555-912-1987
dj@northern-lights-preschool.com

May 18

Dear Mr. and Mrs. Delia,

I want to thank you again for talking to me about Susan. I think she would make an excellent pastry chef at Delia's Trattoria.   As I said, she is a wonderful baker. She has been baking goodies for our school since I arrived. She consistently comes up with ideas that match the theme of our events.   Everyone loves her treats.

Susan is a loving person with an excellent work ethic. She belongs in an environment where she can be both creative and a team player.

Please let me know if you have any other questions.

Sincerely,

DJ

TO: SUSAN BAKER
FROM: DJ
DATE: MAY 18
RE: DELIA'S TRATTORIA

Dear Susan,

Your wish is my command! I just want to let you know that I spoke with Mr. and Mrs. Delia last night, and sent them a glowing recommendation letter about you. I really hope this works out for you. If so, you can count on us coming out there often to try out your new delicacies!

Susan, I am so glad we had the chance to work together this past year. You are a loving, kind and dedicated person whose true calling is as a baker. You already have the name, Ms. Baker, you just needed the job!

All the best,
DJ

May 19

Dear DJ,

Thank you for such a wonderful year. Had I known we would have had this much fun, I might have decided to wait a few more years before retiring! You have brought a new sense of energy, purpose, and community to our school. I've so enjoyed our time together!

I know this has been a very difficult year for you. Nine years ago, I, too, lost my best friend to breast cancer. Donna and I were very much like you and Cheryl. Watching the two of you when you thought you were alone in the garden was touching. Donna and I would spend our time laughing and talking, too. She was my biggest supporter, just like Cheryl was for you. Not a day goes by that I don't think about her and smile. You and Cheryl were lucky to have each other.

As I prepare to leave Northern Lights after 20 years, I want to give something to you and the school that will stay long after I am gone. In light of this past year, in honor of your sister's strength and courage, and in partnership with Deirdre and Grant, I want to plant two rows of Sunflowers in the garden yard, one row for Cheryl and one for Donna. I hope you like it. If so, Joe and I will make the arrangements immediately.

I will never forget this year. You taught me so much about teaching. Where were you 30 years ago when I was just starting out?

Thank you again. What a pleasure it has been to work with you!

With warmest regards,

Kathleen Witherington

(Mrs. W.)

A Note from DJ

May 20

Dear Kathleen, (That is truly a beautiful name!)

Thank you for such a wonderful letter and beautiful gift. As you know from our talks, Cheryl loved sunflowers. Whenever we had the chance to be outside, she would turn her head towards the sun, close her eyes, and take in all the warmth. When we traveled (even in winter), we would rent convertibles just so we could feel the sun on our faces. Cheryl started collecting sunflowers years ago as a reminder of those wonderful warm feelings.

The garden is already a wonderful place for me. Knowing she's been there with me offers a sense of comfort. Whenever I am sitting there I will never be alone. The idea of seeing sunflowers on that yard is overwhelming to me. I can't thank you enough for such a thoughtful gesture.

I have enjoyed working with you this year. Your love and respect for children flows through everything you do. You are a Master teacher. I appreciate all of your support as you quietly showed the teachers, through your classroom experiences, the value of developmentally appropriate practice. You were an integral part of this year's change, and I am forever grateful.

Thank you again for the sunflowers! Please come back and see them next year!

All the best,
DJ

May 24

Hi Mom,

Last night's annual board meeting was great. The Parents Committee wanted the board to know how impressed they were with the changes we've made, so they invited several parents and two teachers to talk about their experiences this past year. They called it a "Power Hour!" How cool is that? Grant talked about everything he's learned this year and how he can't wait to continue this "journey into early learning." Wow! I was impressed to hear him use the language of Reggio-inspired teachers. What a surprise. Jennifer talked about her experience with the photography and shared that she had no idea how she managed to plan for her children before she met me. She said she felt more confident that she is doing what is best for children and was very complimentary about me to the board.

William's mom made me cry when she shared that this is the first year William has gone to school willingly and without problems. She said he had given her a hard time in the mornings for several months, but sometime in late fall he announced that he needed to be at school to see his friends and DJ. She also shared with the group that because of the tweeting and journaling this past year, she found that William loved to draw letters, and found him teaching his little sister some of the letters.

At the end of the evening the board president announced that we will be starting our NAEYC accreditation process in the fall and that they are going to pay for the entire school to go to next year's NAEYC conference in Washington, DC. I wonder how long it will take me to get them to pay for a trip to Reggio Emilia, Italy?

I love this place, Mom. We have a long way to go, but I'm so glad we are on this journey!

PS. They named the Garden yard in a vote last week. Tonight we learned that it's new name will be "The Curious Garden." It's based upon a book we read in the school. Parents loved being involved in the voting, as did the mailman and all the delivery guys!

Hi Mom,

I'm outside, writing from the garden, sitting under the tree again. This time; however, I am sitting on a bench under the tree. A beautiful bench decorated with photos of all the children in the school. On the corner, there is a photo of Cheryl and me. Jennifer took the photo of us (I had no idea) when Cheryl was here last fall. It's beautiful, Mom. I wish you could see it.

Its only June and we are already at 85% capacity for next year! What a great feeling. I was hoping for at least 60% knowing that the Summer is usually when families decide if they are going to re-enroll. Our twos room is almost full. I've registered 8 new children this month alone! Thank goodness for word of mouth advertising and a good reputation!

The teachers seem genuinely excited about the program. They are already talking about fall and how they want to set up their rooms. Several teachers are planning on taking field trips this summer to some schools in the region that have similar practices!

I can see most of the parents are pleased, as well. There will always be the few moms or dads who want to know where the prep school mentality went, but overall, most of the families know that Northern Lights Preschool is where their child is seen as an individual learner with extraordinary capabilities.

I only need to find a few staff for next year. We need someone for the twos room and an assistant for Deirdre. (I'm moving Grant into Mrs. W.'s room as the lead with Kaycee.) Susan Baker, our twos teacher, starts next month as a pastry chef at a local Italian restaurant, and Mrs. W. is on her way to Phoenix to live near her daughter. We brought on a great new cook, Miss Georgia, (Connie has decided to be a stay at home mom) and she is already working on a healthy snack menu for fall and nudging me to start a staff lunch program so we can ALL become healthy eaters. How lucky can I get!?

The rows of sunflowers in the garden have been planted. It looks just like a pile of dirt right now. Hard to believe that will be filled with flowers when the children come back in the fall.

I will have a little down time for about a month before we start gearing up for the fall again. Down time. Wow, I've been working nonstop all year.

I wish I could come visit you.
Love,
DJ

A Note from DJ

May 28

Hi Beth,

School's almost out! I'm still holding my breath, but I think you and I can safely say "We survived our first year in our new schools! Yay us!"

I want to Whoa Nelly you on something. I completely understand why you want to redecorate the rooms over the summer. It's so much easier to do it while the teachers and students aren't there to question (or in some cases, challenge) what you are doing. Plus it's a nice surprise for everyone that the classrooms are set up when school starts. Remember, if your teachers are not involved in the decision making about their rooms, it's only a matter of time before they rearrange the furniture or create a schedule that makes using that environment next to impossible.

Remember that your school is not someone else's baby. You designed it based on your vision and the ideas of your families and teachers. Your teachers need to take ownership of their rooms: the physical set up and their schedules. Doing it for them without their input is not consistent with your vision.

Why not use the next three months to facilitate a conversation between a few teachers, and let them work through why they should make some changes in their classrooms?

You can start with some readings from <u>Caring Spaces, Learning Places</u> by Jim Greenman. Couple that with <u>Reflecting Children's Lives</u> by Margie Carter and Deb Curtis. I successfully used these books in tandem several times with teachers. Once they understand the philosophy behind re-creating their environment and better understand how children learn, then you can take them to a few schools for inspiration. After that, set them free in their classrooms. I assure you their changes will reflect your vision, too!

All in all, I am just so glad that you feel ready to face another year. It's amazing the strength we find within ourselves when it comes to working with children. In the long run, dealing with our worries about pushy parents and stubborn teachers is worth it. Now we can look at our school and see happy children who are focused on important work they helped to create, who know they belong and matter, and who will become creative thinkers and problem solving grown-ups.

It's all good!

Looking forward to getting together this summer!

DJ

Mom, you are not going to believe this!

Graduation was yesterday, and we had a wonderful ceremony in the garden. When we were getting ready to leave, Mrs. W. and the other teachers asked me to wait while they presented the plaque for the garden yard. I was dumbfounded, Mom. She announced: "This garden is being dedicated to two brave sisters who showed us how to fight for what they believed in and never gave up." And in beautiful letters, its name was inscribed:

My Sister's Garden

So now, here I sit, in My Sister's Garden, surrounded by photos of wonderful people, many who are new family to me. Yes, there will be times when I'll be lonely out here, but I'll never be alone. Once the sunflowers bloom and the plaque is put in place, I'll have what I need to continue this journey.

Please take care of Cheryl for me. Tell her I love her and miss her so much.

I'll still write to you both, I promise. And I'll be quiet sometimes, too, in case you want to whisper to me.

I love you Mom,

DJ

A Note To Teachers

"Be the change you wish to see in the world." - Mahatma Ghandi

A teacher who read a preview of Monday Memo told me she wished the book was already published and that her director had the chance to read it. Her concern whas that since she was "only a teacher," she wasn't able to make real change in her school.

Hogwash.
This memo is for you.

Dear Teacher,

You are one of the most important pieces of the preschool puzzle. You are the one responsible for keeping a schedule, maintaining order, scaffolding learning and setting the tone of your classroom. You are the front line when it comes to the parents. If it weren't for you, the directors would be giving tours of an empty school.

All of us deserve to work in a place that respects children and offers them the absolute best early childhood experience. If you feel your program needs some work, please don't back down or give up.

You have rights.

You have the right to work in an environment that reflects joy and learning.

You have the right to professional development that is specifically geared to you and your needs as a teacher.

You have the right to be seen as a competent teacher who is capable of making the right decisions for her students.

You have the right to have co-workers who are professional, collaborative and equally passionate about early childhood education.

Please understand that with those rights come responsibilities. Before you point your finger at your director, take a moment and look at yourself.

You also have responsibilities.

You have the responsibility to make your classroom a space that reflects joy and learning.

You have the responsibility to teach children according to their individual needs.

You have the responsibility to see your children as competent and capable of making choices about their interests.

You have the responsibility to seek professional development that helps you become a teacher who can deliver numbers 1-3.

You have the responsibility to be a co-worker who is professional, collaborative, and equally passionate about early childhood education.

You have a responsibility to have a vision of excellent early childhood education. (If you don't, email me. You can borrow mine until you create your own.)

Decide now to create the best possible classroom you can. The books and articles listed in the references are available online or in bookstores. Read everything you can, find like-minded people, ask questions, go to conferences, join ECE discussion groups, but don't, under any circumstance, allow yourself to do less than what you know is right for children just because your director isn't up to speed yet.

Decide now that you don't need all new materials, better carpets, sleeker furniture and smart boards before you can have a wonderful program.

Decide now to avoid excuses like "I can't do this until my coworkers do."

Stop waiting for others to do what's right for children.

Decide now to become an excellent teacher. We are counting on you.

With utmost respect,

DJ Schneider Jensen

A Note About Staff Meetings

In my early years as a director, staff meetings were long, unorganized, and sometimes hijacked by irate teachers with their own agendas. I have met teachers all around the country who have the same lament. They feel that staff meetings are often laced with negativity or jam packed with so much trivial information there is no time for collaboration. Teachers want to get to know the other people who work in their school, but since they are holed up in their classrooms all day, there is very little time for community building.

Over the years I learned that staff meetings are an excellent way to build community, inspire creativity, and support teacher learning. Be intentional.

What is the purpose of your staff meeting? What messages do you want to send? Are those messages consistent with your vision? Is the bulk of the meeting to share "housekeeping" information, as in "remember to turn in your field trip forms?" If so, consider sending a memo instead. Teachers don't need to listen to repeated rules when in a group setting. They need the opportunity to collaborate.

Do you plan use the meeting as a way to confront only one or two people in the group? If so, decide now to meet with those people at a separate time. The people you want to reach won't hear your message in the meeting anyway. Plus, it is is uncomfortable to watch if you are the teacher who is not in trouble.

When you have asked the entire group to come together, it must be for a reason that affects the crowd. If not, cancel the meeting and meet with small groups of teachers on topics that are relevant to them.

Staff meetings can also be a way to introduce new content/pedagogy to the staff. Consider a book club/article club format, where staff read in advance and come together to share their insights.

And finally, staff gatherings can be a venue for celebrations. Consider monthly opportunities to share what is working in their classroom, so you can celebrate the steps each staff member is taking.

A Note About Reflective Questions

We ask our teachers to be reflective when working with their children. Reflection and introspection help teachers be thoughtful and intentional in their practice.
Model what you expect to see in your school. When you ask reflective questions of your staff, your reinforce your belief in this type of thinking, and show them how to reflect with their students.

When teachers share ideas, ask them to think about their plans:

What caused you to think about this idea?
What is your intent with this activity?
How does this align with the children's interests?
What other options did you consider before this one?
What developmental goals are you hoping to meet?

When there are behavior challenges, use reflection to clarify what is happening:

Why do you think Joey responded like he did?
What are his strengths?
What is he trying to communicate?
What does he love to do?
How can you help him feel comfortable in the classroom?

Use reflective questions to help teachers communicate with families:

What message do you want to send to the parents?
Does sharing this information help the situation?
How does it align with our vision and mission?
What other ways can you communicate this?

The 5 R's of Exceptional Teachers

We've all had a teacher who was good, but not great. We couldn't quite put our finger on what they needed, so we weren't able to support their growth. Once you figure out where a teacher could use support, you are able determine the best way to help.

How you support your teacher is varied. You can choose formal or informal professional development, have her join an ECE book club, team him up with a mentor, or engage in a heart to heart conversation. Regardless of your approach, you will need a clear idea of your goal. This list breaks the characteristics into 5 areas:

RELATIONSHIPS: Exceptional teachers create and maintain positive relationships with families and coworkers.

RESPONSIBILITY: Exceptional teachers take responsibility for his/her professional development by attending informal and formal classes, joining ECE organizations, and by reading ECE books, articles and/or trade magazines.

REFLECTION: Exceptional teachers use reflective questions, observations and developmental checklists to assess children's learning and drive curriculum planning.

RESPECT: Exceptional teachers create and maintain a classroom environment that sparks wonder and curiosity and has a culture of mutual respect.

REGARD: Exceptional teachers show Absolute Intentional Regard for all children using both verbal and non-verbal cues.

A Note About Creating Change

1. Become an expert on your vision.

The first step to creating change is understanding the direction you are headed. If you are interested in becoming a child-centered program, you will need to have a solid understanding of how children learn, developmentally appropriate practice, and assessment goals for each age group. Creating change involves leading and inspiring people. Cheerleading will only work for so long. As your staff begins practicing their new skills, they will have questions and unless you have answers (or access to answers) you won't be able to support them.

A few years ago, I was speaking about change to directors at an NAEYC conference. I wish I could have videotaped the audience. Their faces showed interest as I introduced the topic of change, then full engagement as we discussed the benefits of child-led learning, then confusion as they began to reflect how they would apply this in their school, followed by fear as they imagined the questions their teachers and parents would ask; questions for which they had no answers. I offered them a scenario to consider (below). Their answers helped them gauge their knowledge of child-centered learning. How do you fare on the questions?

- A fours teacher tells you that she really thinks worksheets and letters of the week are the only way to teach language and literacy. How do you convince her otherwise?
- A parent asks you to use time out with her son whenever he misbehaves. How do you explain why time out is not an option at your school?
- A threes teacher takes the easel and/or sand table out of her classroom, stating they are too messy and the children can't seem to use them properly. How do you explain the value of these materials?
- A teacher has taken all of the musical instruments out of reach of the children stating she prefers giving it to them occasionally since they get really noisy. How do you explain the importance of individual musical experiences?
- A frustrated teacher asks you how to get the children to do more than just scribble. She wants to go back to projects because "at least they can take home something." How do you handle her frustration?
- Once a teacher has your vision and sees a connection, they are ready to test their wings. Give them the opportunity to use their newfound skills. This is where good management skills pay off.

2. Share the Vision, and Teach the Steps.

Knowing what you want is half the battle. There is comfort in knowing what you are working towards. Weight Watchers has this concept mastered. They tell you what your goal is then encourage you to lose 10%. Not all of it – 10%. When you get off the wagon, (and they expect you to) they offer support and tips.

As you move your staff towards a child-centered, emergent learning approach, remember that they will have fear and anxiety and are bound to make mistakes. Just make sure your teachers are moving forward. When they do, a few may move in baby steps. That's perfectly fine. Celebrate the successes!

The order of the steps changes depending on the teacher's level of experience and prior knowledge. Every teacher needs to understand DAP. After that, the next steps are observation, documentation, assessment, reflection and communication.

Some directors try to teach the entire group the same step at the same time. That can be a counterintuitive plan for an approach that works with the individual child. A great rule of thumb is "model exactly what you expect from your teachers." Teach with the tenets of developmentally appropriate practice in mind.

Understand how each teacher learns, what motivates them, and their skills and talents. To do this, you will need to observe your teachers. Watch them in action. See how they handle drop off, circle time, transitions, center time, etc. Keep notes on each teacher.

Use this knowledge to guide their learning. For some teachers, you may offer research articles and studies; for others you may offer lighter reading. Some teachers do better if they can see DAP/emergent learning/Reggio-inspired approach in action and will benefit from field trips to other programs. There are online videos available, too. My favorite is *Videatives.com*. George and his team are exceptional at finding just the right videos to depict how young children think.

3. Help your staff find their connection.

Children are always seeking connections: "How does this relate to what I know?" "Why is this important?" "What's in it for me?" This is the same for adults who are asked to try something new. Think about life before the smartphones. "I'm fine with my flip phone" can be translated as "This thing is so hard and makes no sense. Why would I want to use the internet from this?" If you want to make a change, you'll need to make connections.

For some teachers, the connections will come easily. Share research about what is best for children, and you'll have several staff on board right away. For others, you may have to draw out the connection for them. Listen as they share stories about their students and find clues that you can use to make the connection. For example, in Monday Memo, DJ's conversation with Deirdre about her becoming a Kindergarten teacher may have served as the catalyst for Deirdre's reflection of her practice.

For other teachers, you have to work harder on making a connection. Deirdre was unwilling to make a connection at first, which explains why she was having a difficult time. Her realization was that making children early readers like Shannon wasn't creating well-rounded adults. When she made that connection, she was able to move forward.

4. Give them a chance to fly.

Once a teacher has your vision and sees a connection, they are ready to test their wings. Give them the opportunity to use their newfound skills. This is where good management skills kick in. For some of us, this is going to be the hardest part.

Intentionally giving a staff member autonomy can be scary, responsible decisions generally are. However, once you understand how the teacher views the children in her classroom and how she approaches learning, you will have a better gauge. Make sure she understands your vision. Never walk away from your vision. Guide your teacher using your vision. Model what you believe. You can do this. Go you!

I applaud you for taking the journey towards a developmentally appropriate school that offers excellent care and education. Please let me know how I may be of continued service to you or to join me for online classes.

Email playforaliving@gmail.com.
Twitter: @playforaliving.
Facebook: DJ.Jensen

Questions for Group Discussion

Communities of practice, also known professional learning communities, are made up of professionals with similar missions. If your school or community has not yet created one, consider this concept. Once a month teachers/directors meet to discuss topics, books, and question that affect their practice. In my current practice, this list serves as ice breaker questions whenever I meet with teachers or directors. Below is a sample list of questions to start the conversations.

For Directors:

How can you/do you support fellow directors?

What do you look for when you observe/hire teachers?

What is the best way a colleague could support you?

What are some of the characteristics of memorable ECE teachers in your life?

What are the indicators that your staff meetings are out of control?

Would you prefer communicating with your staff via memos/emails or face to face? Why?

What are your school's values? How do you communicate it to teachers and parents?

How do you manage confidentiality and improper sharing of personal information?

What does "academic results" mean to you? Is that consistent with how your teachers view academic results?

How do you/how does your school manage sadness and loss?

How do you feel about/what are your experiences with specials?

How do you model/practice building relationships at your school?

How do you model/teach DAP?

What is your philosophy on classroom setup?

How do you know that it's time to make a change and let a teacher go?

What are some ways you get to know your teachers and make yourself present in conversations with them?

How do you handle parent conferences at your school?

How do you make the process of change relevant to each teacher?

How do you handle graduation/moving up ceremonies at your school?

How do you handle separation anxiety at your school?

For Directors and Teachers:

Are you developmentally appropriate? What are some examples you can share?

What does intentional mean? What examples do you have of intentionally setting up materials to capture children's interest?

What is your philosophy for teaching children?

How do you feel about free play?

How do you manage the relationship between your personal and professional lives?

Should time out be used in a classroom? Under what circumstances?

Do you practice Absolute Intentional Regard? Share examples.

What is your first inclination when a child "acts out."

How can you incorporate technology in your classroom?

How do you provide evidence to families that "learning" is happening?

How do you feel about using worksheets?

What are your experiences with Parent Nights?

What advice do you have for teachers in schools where the director "doesn't get it"?

A Note About My Sister

For years I would tell people, "My sister, Cheryl, is just like me, only prettier." Turns out she would tell her friends, "My sister, DJ, is just like me, only funnier." We were 3 years, 3 months and 3 days apart. I adored her and was jealous of her, all at the same time. She had a beautiful smile and long straight hair that she would pile on the top of her head and pin to an empty Coke can before going to bed. (I had short curly hair and a terrible overbite.) We had our share of sibling rivalry, too. She pushed me into a bed once during a fight over who was going to empty the dishwasher. I ended up with 22 stitches on my tush. (But I didn't have to empty the dishwasher! Booyah!)

We sang all the time. Broadway tunes, The Carpenters, you name it, we belted it out. We would play a little game when we were bored; going through the alphabet, picking shows or songs in ABC order and singing them. If we got stuck, we would giggle and pretend that letter didn't exist. Giggling was our thing. Out of the blue, we would look at each other and without saying a word we'd start giggling. I loved that. I miss that.

Cheryl loved the work I was doing. She was my biggest cheerleader; reminding me how important early childhood education was and how lucky I was to find my life's calling so early on. Whenever the demands of this business became overwhelming, I would call Cheryl, either crying or venting, and she would listen; offering the appropriate "how dare her" or "you've got to be kidding me" at the perfect time. When I was done, she would help me determine another approach and would tell me to go back and try it again. Her support was never-ending.

Cheryl found a lump in her left breast over the winter of 2008. In mid January, we learned this 'alien' had a name: Triple Negative Breast Cancer. We also learned that Cheryl had the BRCA gene which can be found among Eastern European Jews. A month later, she had had begun the process of fighting with all her might. Surgeries. Chemo. Radiation. More Surgeries. More Chemo. After her diagnosis, I learned I had the same BRCA gene and elected to have my surgeries prophylactically. We timed them so that I could come to her for her procedures and then she would come to me for mine.

Sometime during the first few months of this journey, Cheryl and her friends decided to join the Komen 3 Day. She later told me it was something that she could control and she wanted to help others with breast cancer. She called me up and announced "Guess what? I'm gonna walk 60 miles over 3 days! And you are, too!"

We walked that Summer, in oppressive Cleveland heat. Cheryl was the only walker who was currently undergoing chemo treatments. What an amazing woman! We walked 47 miles that year, 60 the next, and 60 the next. (She also found time to be on the Cleveland crew that third year, too!) At that third walk, during the opening ceremonies, we heard the spokeswoman announce that Komen had funded millions for research for Triple Negative Breast Cancer. Cheryl looked over at me, beaming, and said, "I'm so glad we're walking! Look at where the money is going!" We had no idea that those funds would actually be responsible for the clinical trial she underwent 6 months later.

For Chanukah in 2011, we pampered ourselves. Her massage therapist surprised us by questioning a lump she found. Walking into 2012 looked so scary. We decided to make EMPOWERMENT our word for the year.

From January through August 2012, Cheryl was a woman on a mission. She danced at her daughter's wedding, watched her son graduate college, and was there for the birth of her first grandchild. She wrote an inspiring CaringBridge blog and created a Facebook group for TNBC survivors. She jumped at the chance to join a clinical trial. When her nurse learned about Cheryl's commitment to Komen, she told her that the trial was made possible by the funds from Komen. Cheryl took that as a good sign. Whenever she was sick from the treatment and we suggested she discontinue the trial, she would tell us, "If they learn something because I participated in this trial, then my death won't be in vain."

We lost Cheryl just 13 days after her grandson was born. From generation to generation. He's beautiful. He has her nose. And he loves to giggle.

Cheryl and I talked a lot about writing a book for women. Self-esteem and body image, living a purposeful life, success in business. Regardless of the topic, the message was always the same: See your value and love yourself.

Well, Sister, we did it!

References

Cadwell, Louise Boyd. Bringing Reggio Emilia home: an innovative approach to early childhood education. New York: Teachers College Press, 1997. Print.

Carter, Margie, and Debbie Curtis. Spreading the news: sharing the stories of early childhood education. St. Paul, MN: Redleaf Press;, 1996. Print.

Carter, Margie, and Debbie Curtis. The visionary director: a handbook for dreaming, organizing, and improvising in your center. 2nd ed. St. Paul, MN: Redleaf Press, 2010. Print.

Chenfeld, Mimi Brodsky. Teaching in the key of life: a collection of the writings of Mimi Brodsky Chenfeld.. Washington: National Association for the Education of Young Children, 1993. Print.

Copple, Carol, and Sue Bredekamp. Basics of developmentally appropriate practice: an introduction for teachers of children 3 to 6. Washington, DC: National Association for the Education of Young Children, 2006. Print.

Cryer, Debby, Thelma Harms, and Cathy Riley. All about the ECERS-R: a detailed guide in words and pictures to be used with the ECERS-R. (Lewisville, NC): Pact House Pub., 2003. Print.

Curtis, Debbie, and Margie Carter. The art of awareness: how observation can transform your teaching. St. Paul, MN: Redleaf Press, 2000. Print.

Curtis, Debbie, and Margie Carter. Designs for living and learning: transforming early childhood environments. St. Paul, MN: Redleaf Press, 2003. Print.

Curtis, Debbie, and Margie Carter. Learning together with young children: a curriculum framework for reflective teachers. St. Paul, MN: Redleaf Press, 2008. Print.

Curtis, Debbie, and Margie Carter. Reflecting children's lives: a handbook for planning your child-centered curriculum. 2nd ed. St. Paul, MN: Redleaf Press, 2011. Print.

Editors, National Association for the Education of Young Children, and International Reading Association Editors. "Learning to Read and Write: Developmentally Appropriate Practices for Young Children." young children 53.4 (1998): 30-46. Print. Position Statement

Edwards, Carolyn P., Lella Gandini, and George E. Forman. The hundred languages of children: the Reggio Emilia approach to early childhood education. Norwood, N.J.: Ablex Pub. Corp., 1993. Print.

Epstein, Ann S.. The intentional teacher: choosing the best strategies for young children's learning. Washington, DC: National Association for the Education of Young Children, 2007. Print.

Galinsky, Ellen. Mind in the making: the seven essential life skills every child needs. New York: HarperStudio, 2010. Print.

Gardner, Howard. Intelligence reframed: multiple intelligences for the 21st century. New York, NY: Basic Books, 1999. Print.

Goleman, Daniel. Emotional intelligence . New York: Bantam Books, 1995. Print.

Gonzalez-Mena, Janet . "Compassionate roots begin with babies." Child Care Information Exchange May 2010: 46-49. Print.

Gopnik, Alison, Andrew N. Meltzoff, and Patricia K. Kuhl. The scientist in the crib: what early learning tells us about the mind. New York: Perennial, 2001. Print.

Greenman, James T.. Caring spaces, learning places: children's environments that work. Redmond, WA: Exchange Press, 1988. Print.

Grover, Ron. The Disney touch: Disney, ABC & the quest for the world's greatest media empire. rev. ed. Chicago: Irwin, 1997. Print.

Harms, Thelma, Richard M. Clifford, and Debby Cryer. Early childhood environment rating scale . Rev. ed. New York: Teachers College Press, 1998. Print.

Helm, Judy Harris, and Lilian G. Katz. Young investigators: the project approach in the early years. New York: Teachers College Press, 2001. Print.

Hyson, Marilou. Enthusiastic and engaged learners: approaches to learning in the early childhood classroom. New York: Teachers College Press; 2008. Print.

Jensen, DJ Schneider. How to eat an elephant. Baltimore, MD: Self-pub. 2006

Jensen, DJ Schneider. TIMME, time management made easy. Baltimore, MD: Self-pub. 2005

Jensen, DJ Schneider. Trainer's guide to training, Las Vegas, NV: Self-pub. 2000

Johnson, Spencer. Who moved my cheese?: an amazing way to deal with change in your work and in your life. New York: Putnam, 1998. Print.

Katz, Lilian G., and Sylvia C. Chard. Engaging children's minds: the project approach. Norwood, N.J.: Ablex Pub. Corp., 1989. Print.

Kohn, Alfie. Punished by rewards: the trouble with gold stars, incentive plans, A's, praise, and other bribes. Boston: Houghton Mifflin Co., 1993. Print.

Losardo, Angela, and Angela Syverson. Alternative approaches to assessing young children . Baltimore: Paul H. Brookes Pub. Co., 2001. Print.

Nash, J. Madeline. "Fertile Minds." time 3 Feb. 1997: 22-28. Print.

Noddings, Nel. "What does it mean to educate the whole child?." Educational Leadership September 2005 (2005): 8-13. Print.

Olfman, Sharna. Child honoring: how to turn this world around. Westport, CT: Praeger Publishers, 2006. Print.

Paley, Vivian Gussin. The boy who would be a helicopter . Cambridge, Mass.: Harvard University Press, 1990. Print.

Paley, Vivian Gussin. A child's work: the importance of fantasy play. Chicago: University of Chicago Press, 2004. Print.

Pasek, Kathy, Roberta M. Golinkoff, and Diane E. Eyer. Einstein never used flash cards: how our children really learn--and why they need to play more and memorize less. Emmaus, PA.: Rodale; 2003. Print.

Phillips, Deborah, and Fred A. Bernstein. How to give your child a great self-image. London: Penguin Books, 1991. Print.

Seitz, Hilary. "The power of documentation in the early childhood classroom." young children March 2008 (2008): 88-93. www.naeyc.org. Web. 2 May 2009.

Shore, Rima. Rethinking the brain: new insights into early development. New York: Families and Work Institute, 1997. Print.

Slavin, R.E.. Educational research in an age of accountability. Boston: Pearson Education, 2007. Print.

"Vermont's Statewide Report on Kindergarten Readiness 2009-2010." www.education.vermont.gov.

Wheeler, Edyth J. Conflict resolution in early childhood: helping children understand and resolve conflicts. Upper Saddle River, N.J.: Pearson Education, 2004. Print.

Wien, Carol Anne. Negotiating standards in the primary classroom: the teacher's dilemma. New York: Teachers College Press, 2004. Print.

Wurm, Julianne. Working in the Reggio way: a beginner's guide for American teachers. St. Paul, MN: Redleaf Press, 2005. Print.

Zigler, Edward, Matia Stevenson, and Nancy Wilson Hall. The first three years & beyond: brain development and social policy. New Haven: Yale University Press, 2002. Print.